# SEW
## *many*
# DRESSES,
### *sew little time*

# SEW *many* DRESSES, *sew little time*

### *the ultimate* DRESSMAKING GUIDE

*interchangeable patterns*
*to* **CREATE 200+**
**UNIQUE DRESSES**

*Tanya Whelan*

POTTER
CRAFT

NEW YORK

Published in the United States by Potter Craft, an imprint
of the Crown Publishing Group, a division of Random
House LLC, a Penguin Random House Company,
New York.
www.crownpublishing.com
www.pottercraft.com

POTTER CRAFT and colophon are registered trademarks
of Random House LLC.

Library of Congress Cataloging-in-Publication Data
Whelan, Tanya.
  Sew many dresses, sew little time: the ultimate
dressmaking guide: interchangeable patterns to create
200+ unique dresses / Tanya Whelan. -- First Edition.
    pages cm
(alk. paper)
1. Dressmaking. I. Title.
  TT519.5.W44 2015
  646.4--dc23
        2014040704

ISBN 978-0-7704-3494-6
eISBN 978-0-7704-3495-3

Printed in China

Photographs by Tanya Whelan
Illustrations by Tanya Whelan, Barry Becker,
and Barbie McCormick
Technical and editorial contributions by
Barbie McCormick
Styling and dressmaking by Tanya Whelan and
Sandra Hutton
Jacket design by Stephanie Huntwork
Jacket photograph by Tanya Whelan

10 9 8 7 6 5 4 3 2 1

First Edition

TO MY MOTHER-IN-LAW, MAXINE WENDELKEN, the most glamorous and beautiful woman I ever met in real life, and an expert dressmaker and designer in her own right. Those pictures of you in those beautiful dresses that you made yourself have always mesmerized me and helped motivate me to write this book. Thank you for inspiring me, Maxine. I love you.

# CONTENTS

# *introduction*

Making a dress is not hard! In fact, making a dress is often more straightforward than making a handbag. And with the interchangeable patterns in this book, designing and creating hundreds of unique looks—219 dresses, to be exact—is well within reach.

The secret is that the waist darts and measurements line up perfectly with each bodice and skirt in this collection, making the patterns completely interchangeable. As someone who has sewn from individual dress patterns for years, I must admit to being a little embarrassed not to have realized earlier that a system of interchangeable bodice and skirt patterns was a possibility.

Fitted dresses with waist seams actually all share the same basic construction, so theoretically, you should be able to switch the bodice of any fitted dress pattern to the skirt of another pattern. But in reality, you would probably have to make a few changes to the patterns, such as moving the waist darts and altering the waist width. I wanted to make this process easy-peasy, so I created a set of basic patterns for bodices and skirts that meet perfectly at the waist to be combined and interchanged according to your dressmaking instincts. Instead of simply sewing from patterns, I want you to know that you can indeed design your own dresses, customized with the silhouette and fit that you desire.

Even experienced sewers are sometimes nervous about the idea of making a dress for themselves. After all, unlike an accessory, a quilt, or a home-decorating item, a dress is something you actually wear on your body out in the world. I think many sewers have the sense that dressmaking is too difficult or requires a very specialized knowledge of sewing, and that whatever they make is going to end up looking "homemade" so the whole dressmaking business is best left to professionals or very experienced sewers. But there's no need to fear! In past generations it was very common for home sewers to make their own dresses. In high schools across the country, home ec classes taught the basics of sewing and clothing construction so people knew that making clothing was something the average person could—and should—do. If you've ever checked out the inside of dresses from a vintage shop you'll see that many of them don't have labels and were in fact made by home sewers. I can't actually remember seeing a dress in a vintage shop and thinking, "Boy, that looks homemade." Usually I'm just thinking about the design, the cut, the fabrics, and the finishing techniques used in the garment.

When I started writing this book, I had a conversation with my mother-in-law, who was a professional designer, seamstress, and incredibly stylish lady in New York City in the '60s, about the revelation that sewing a dress is really so much easier than people today think it is. She agreed that women used to make dresses all the time and women today could do it, too. She later showed me pictures of herself looking totally *Mad Men* '60s glam in beautiful, simple, and classic fitted sheath dresses she had made herself. Talk about inspiration.

If you know how to use a sewing machine and want to design and sew your own dresses, this book is for you. Advanced beginners will find simple step-by-step patterns and instructions to make beautiful, classic dresses. For competent sewers who have sewn with patterns before, the book offers a complete set of dependable interchangeable bodice and skirt patterns that add up to 219 possible unique dresses. If you are curious about pattern design, there are simple techniques for modifying patterns. Do you want to learn to alter a pattern to fit your figure better? This book covers that as well.

Ultimately, I hope that *Sew Many Dresses* helps you to make a beautiful dress (better yet, an entire wardrobe of dresses), following your own sense of design, that you feel wonderful in.

## HOW TO USE THIS BOOK

More than 200 unique dresses can be made with the interchangeable bodice and skirt patterns, neckline templates, and sleeve patterns included in the envelope at back of the book. Each project includes instructions and illustrations for the individual pattern piece as well as steps to join the skirts to the bodices and the bodices to the sleeves. In addition to the enclosed patterns, I

also provide step-by-step tutorials to make easy patterns for circle skirts, gathered, and pleated skirts, as well as a variety of collars. Throughout the book, Pattern Design Spotlights show you how to move darts around the bodice, change darts to gathers, and create fullness in bodices and skirts. These simple techniques open up a huge number of possible dress designs in addition to the 219 combinations using just the patterns and templates.

All of the pattern pieces are timeless, versatile designs that, depending on the chosen combination and fabric, can be used to make a dress that reflects your personality, whether it's the Vintage-Style Rockabilly Dress (page 80) or the classic Day-to-Evening Sheath (page 49). These patterns will allow you to re-create many of your favorite looks, as so many ready-to-wear dresses are made with this simple construction of a bodice sewn to a skirt at the waist. The possibilities are truly exciting.

Finally, a book about fitted dresses wouldn't be complete without a section on alterations. After all, if the dress doesn't fit your specific individual figure, it doesn't do you much good, no matter how lovely the design may be. In order to address some common fitting problems, I've included a basic guide to altering the patterns in this book.

# ·1·

## sewing essentials

BEFORE DIVING INTO THE PATTERNS, IT'S IMPORTANT FOR US TO review the basics of dressmaking, from stocking your sewing space with tools and supplies, to choosing fabrics, to cutting and assembling the final garment. As you read the project instructions, you'll see many references back to this section. It's a great place to start, but also to refresh your memory about a specific method or process.

This chapter covers all the basic tools and supplies that you'll need to complete the projects in this book. There's also a guide to understanding fabrics: how to choose, prepare, and care for them. Basic stitches you'll use for dressmaking are reviewed here as well. In addition to basic sewing techniques used for dressmaking, this chapter also covers the basics of understanding pattern markings, how to make facings, assemble a garment with a lining, insert a zipper, and pad a dress form to your own measurements to achieve a better fit in your final dress. The chapter ends with a handy checklist to review before starting your dress.

# TOOLS AND SUPPLIES

To make the dresses in this book you will need the basic tools required for any sewing project plus a few more, explained in this section.

**Sewing machine.** Any basic model will do. I use a very inexpensive machine, and it works just fine.

**Tracing paper.** Large sheets if possible for tracing the patterns. Or, you can use a see-through shower curtain and trace the patterns using a very fine Sharpie marker.

**Tape.** Used to attach tracing paper together when drafting or altering patterns.

**Serger.** This machine is helpful if you plan to sew with knits. There are a couple of dresses in the book sewn from ponte, a double-knit fabric that, unlike most knits, has enough body that it can be used for fitted dresses. If you don't have a serger, you can substitute a woven fabric that has a bit of spandex in it and use your regular machine. Or use your regular machine to sew knits using a small zigzag stitch and a ballpoint needle.

**Sewing machine needles.** You'll need universal, or basic all-purpose needles, plus a ballpoint needle for sewing knits and a variety of machine needles for light/delicate, medium-, and heavy-weight fabrics.

**Invisible-zipper presser foot.** Though you can actually sew an invisible zipper effectively using a regular zipper foot (truth be told, I often do), an invisible-zipper foot is helpful for inserting invisible zippers as it allows you to get very close to the zipper teeth. Though most machines come with a regular zipper foot, they don't usually come with an invisible-zipper foot. You can usually buy a plastic one that works with most machines wherever invisible zippers are sold, though plastic feet are not nearly as

sturdy as metal ones. You can find a metal foot that is compatible with your particular sewing machine online or by contacting your machine's manufacturer.

**Hand-sewing needles.** Various sizes will allow you to baste fabrics and hand-hem skirts.

**Thread.** Choose thread that matches the dominant color in your fabric. All-purpose polyester thread is the best choice for sewing dresses as it's strong and has a bit of flexibility—in other words, it won't break when stretched a bit.

**Pins and pincushion.** I find pearl-tipped pins easier to work with, but regular pins work just fine. Silk pins are very thin and are used for silk and other delicate fabrics.

**Safety pins.** For turning small pieces, such as straps, inside out.

**Good fabric shears.** It is really worth spending the money for a good pair of shears and having them professionally sharpened when needed. They make cutting so much easier and more accurate. Don't use your good shears to cut anything else!

**Regular scissors.** Use these for cutting paper patterns.

**Seam ripper.** Remove temporary basting stitches or sewing mistakes with this tool.

**Pinking shears.** The zigzag blade helps to prevent the raw edges of a seam from fraying.

**Yardstick.** Keep one on hand for measuring fabric yardage and drafting patterns.

**L square or T square.** Any ruler that will allow you to check right angles will also work. In a pinch, you can use a piece of paper instead.

**Soft tape measure.** This tool is essential for taking accurate personal or dress-form measurements.

**Armhole curve ruler, or French curve (optional).** This measures and marks armholes in bodice patterns.

**Hip curve ruler (optional).** Use this to measure and mark curves for skirts.

**Clear ruler (optional).** If you are altering patterns or creating a variation of a pattern, the instructions may call for a ruler or straightedge.

**Tailor's chalk or chalk pencils.** Transfer nonpermanent markings from the patterns to the fabric with either tool.

**Dressmaker's pencil.** You can get a sharper, more accurate line than with chalk using these pencils. The markings can be brushed off or removed with a damp cloth.

**Steam iron.** You will frequently need an iron to press open seams.

**Tailor's ham (optional).** This is very handy for pressing curved areas of a garment such as darts, princess seams, and the shoulders of sleeves, but a rolled hand towel can also be used in place of this professional tool.

## FABRICS

The best way to learn about fabrics is to go to a store that sells a large variety of garment fabrics. Nothing beats seeing and touching fabric to understand its qualities and how it will look when sewn to make a dress. If you're lucky enough to have a good local store, it's worth a visit to get a basic understanding of dressmaking materials. Unfortunately, this is becoming more and more difficult to do as home garment sewing

is just not as common as it used to be. Even the big chain sewing stores, however, will usually carry some variety of basic apparel fabrics.

Compare different fabrics, noting the fiber content, drape, weight, and texture, and imagine what kind of dress would work best with each. This is probably pretty intuitive for you, because even if you have never sewn your own clothes, you have bought and worn clothes and have a sense of what fabrics work for an evening gown, casual or business attire, tailored or flowing garments. I've found that stores with a good selection of fashion fabrics will often have very experienced and passionate sewers working there. Don't be afraid to ask about a particular fabric: What is it usually used for? How difficult or easy is it to work with? Does it require special sewing techniques, needles, or cleaning methods?

If you're unable to check fabrics out in person you can of course shop online, and many of those online stores sell inexpensive swatches. Though you won't be able to get a complete sense of the drape of a fabric from a small swatch, you can still usually get a pretty good idea whether the fabric will work for your planned dress. It makes sense to get a swatch first, especially when buying expensive fabric, as fabric is often not returnable.

Before you purchase fabric, ask yourself this: Will this work for the dress I want to make? For example, you wouldn't choose a heavy wool for a slinky evening dress, a shiny satin for a summer picnic dress, or a sheer georgette for a business dress. Simply put, you want the fabric you're using to look good and to be able to achieve the design you want to create. Consider the occasion (business, formal, casual), time of year (how warm or cool you want to be), and silhouette (slinky and drapey or stiff and constructed) to help you to choose an appropriate fabric.

And never skimp on quality. The fabric doesn't necessarily have to be expensive—in fact, most of the dresses in this book were made with inexpensive yet quality fabric. You will be

putting a lot of time and effort into your new dresses, and it would be a shame to have the effect spoiled by poor fabric. If you have a small budget, look in the remnants or in the clearance sections for lower prices on better goods. With that in mind, here are some factors to think about when choosing fabric:

Fiber. Every fabric has two parts to its name—a fiber and a weave. Fiber is the fabric's content, which can be natural like wool, cotton, silk, and linen, or man-made from natural fibers such as rayon, or synthetic like polyester, nylon, and acrylic. Understanding fiber content will help you determine the warmth, breathability, and cleaning requirements of your finished dress.

Natural-fiber fabrics tend to be more expensive than their synthetic or blended counterparts. If you are new to fabric shopping, read the labels carefully. See if it says "silk" as opposed to "silkies"; the word *silkies* usually refers to a blended fabric that feels similar to silk but is not actually silk. Fiber content is always listed in percentages on the end of the bolt, such as "65 percent cotton, 35 percent polyester." Natural fibers will always handle better than their blended or synthetic counterparts. They are worth the extra cost in the trouble they will save you, and in the finished result.

(continued on page 20)

# *fabrics*

When shopping for fabrics, consider the environment where you will wear your new dress. These are some of the common (and not so common) fabrics that you will find, organized by general occasion.

## EVENING DRESSES

**Silk.** A natural fiber, silk is often smooth and shiny with beautiful drape, but it can be hard to work with. Silk is not always shiny or drapey, however. Dupioni and taffeta, for example, have a stiff hand, and silk tweeds handle almost like cotton or wool.

**Satin.** Usually smooth and very shiny with beautiful drape, satin is somewhat difficult to sew with as it is quite slippery. Matte satins are heavier and easier to work with, but they have less drape. Silk satin is simpler to handle than polyester satin of the same weight.

**Georgette.** Georgette is a lightweight, semisheer fabric with a crepe texture. Due to its lightness, it can be difficult to sew with.

**Crepe.** Crepe can be made of natural or synthetic yarns and comes in different weights, from super lightweight and sheer silk chiffon to heavy wool crepe coating. Four-ply silk crepe is a very luxurious fabric with a soft sheen. It has a crinkly texture and generally a nice drape, plus it's fairly easy to sew with. Crepe shapes easily and has a fair amount of give, so it is comfortable to wear. It's great for sewing bias-cut garments because of its stability. Even wool crepe makes a lovely cocktail dress.

**Lace.** An evening or cocktail dress can be wonderfully elegant in lace. Lace can be made of natural or synthetic fibers and may have spandex added for stretch. Because you can see through it, a lining or underlining is necessary.

**Charmeuse.** Often used in nighties or pajamas, this is what most people think of as "silk." It is a very soft, fluid, shiny satin. The best charmeuse is made from silk and is also readily available in polyester. The silk is easier to work with and makes a wonderful gown or a luxurious lining.

**Chiffon.** Chiffon is very thin and sheer with a beautiful drape. Small needles must be used, and great care must be taken in all steps, since it is easily distorted.

**Crepe de Chine.** This lightweight, beginner-friendly crepe is made from silk (also found in polyester) and has beautiful drape.

**Dupioni silk.** This crisp silk, with body and slubbed texture, is fairly easy to sew with.

**Faille.** Lightweight with a slight luster and ribbed texture that makes it not too difficult to sew with, faille can be made from silk, cotton, or synthetic fibers.

**Habotai.** Also known as China silk, it's not the easiest to sew with, but being thin and lightweight makes it a nice lining or underlining.

**Matelassé.** This double-layer fabric is woven in such a way that the top layer forms a raised pattern, almost giving the appearance of being quilted. In silk or wool, it is very soft. In cotton, it has a firmer hand and a structured drape. Either way, matelassé is fairly easy to work with.

**Organza.** A sheer, stiff fabric made from silk or polyester, organza is great for overlays and underlining.

**Shantung.** Very similar to dupioni, shantung has a smoother texture with only faint slubs.

**Taffeta.** A very firm, stiffly woven silk or poly, it is good for structured garments and full skirts. It is prone to puckered seams if the sewer isn't careful. Fun fact: Taffeta's characteristic rustling sound is called *scroop*.

**Chantilly lace.** A very fine, flat lace, this fabric usually has a floral design and a very fine net background. Named from the region in France where it originated, real Chantilly lace is made with silk or linen and is very expensive. Many imitations abound, generally made from poly, nylon, or rayon. It is very delicate and snags easily, so care must be taken to ensure that the garment will be durable.

**Alençon lace.** A heavy, corded lace, its substantial dimensions and sturdiness help hide flaws and hand-sewing. With both Chantilly and Alençon lace, look for the "eyelashes" on the edges of the scallops; the real French laces will have these hanging free. If the eyelashes are connected with netting or missing altogether, it is a synthetic, machine-made lace, which is less expensive than the imports and often fairly good quality.

## OFFICE DRESSES

**Wool.** Wool is a wonderful fiber to both sew and wear. It comes in many different weaves, weights, and knits; presses like a dream; and is breathable and never clammy. A pair of wool trousers worn in the summer will feel more comfortable than a pair of polyester trousers. Tropical-weight wools are very thin and smooth, perfect for even the hottest, most humid climates. Wool flannel is nice and cozy for colder days. And wool coating will tailor beautifully into an overcoat. Wool fibers naturally have some elasticity, so all wool fabrics will have some give to them.

**Ponte.** A smooth, firm, double-knit fabric, most pontes are mid- to lightweight and, because of their stability, are fairly easy to work with.

**Cotton.** A wonderful fabric for comfort and versatility, cotton is easy to clean, easy to find, and easy to sew and press. Fairly inexpensive, it comes in an infinite variety of weaves, knits, textures, and weights.

**Rayon.** Sometimes known as "imitation silk," rayon is a man-made fiber created from cellulose and cotton, wood, or even bamboo pulp. It has a beautiful, languid drape and either a shiny or matte surface. Medium and heavier weights are not hard to sew with, but the lighter weights and some of the light knits can be tricky to handle. Once known for Hawaiian shirts and '80s peasant skirts, rayon has seen a surge in popularity recently and is often used by itself or as a blend in ready-to-wear garments.

**Twill.** This sturdy weave, common in cotton, wool, and silk, has an identifiable diagonal rib. Most denim is a twill weave. The steeper the diagonal (when looking at the fabric lengthwise), the sturdier and more durable the fabric.

**Gabardine.** Easy to handle and press, gabardine is a type of twill weave, which has more weft (crosswise) yarns than warp (lengthwise) yarns. It is often made from wool but is also available in cottons or synthetics. Wool gabardine is popular for suits and dresses, as it is stain and water resistant.

**Piqué.** Usually made from cotton, or sometimes silk, piqué has a small woven texture of various designs, such as a basket weave or a bird's-eye. Its firm, crisp, yet pliable hand makes it easy to sew and is excellent for dress shirts or jackets.

**Poplin.** A sturdy, plain weave with a crisp hand, this medium- to heavyweight woven cotton is pretty easy to sew, but its stiffness doesn't lend itself to easing or gathering.

**Broadcloth.** A plain-woven, medium-light fabric, broadcloth is very easy to sew. It's often found as a cotton or cotton-poly blend. It was originally named because it was the first cloth to be woven on so-called wide looms, at 45" (114cm), which is now the standard width for garment fabric.

**Silk tweed.** Spun with large, textural yarns, this is similar in appearance to wool tweed, but lighter in weight.

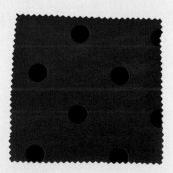

Flocked taffeta

## CASUAL DRESSES

**Cotton.** A wonderful and versatile fiber. Think of your sturdiest jeans, and your softest T-shirt; they are both made from cotton. The easiest cotton to sew is a firm, plain-woven fabric. It won't distort randomly, it feeds readily under the sewing machine, and it presses quite easily.

**Voile.** A very lightweight, mostly sheer fabric, of plain weave, voile can be difficult to handle because of its airiness. Usually you will find it as a cotton variety, but sometimes silk or synthetics are available.

**Batiste.** This very thin, lightweight fabric has a plain weave but is heavier than voile. Because it's usually made from cotton or a cotton-poly blend, it is fairly easy to sew with and works wonderfully as a lining in summer clothes.

**Linen.** Made from the flax plant, linen is very durable, strong, and easy to work with. There is very little give in the fibers, and in drier climates, it wrinkles a lot so it is often blended with cotton or rayon to reduce wrinkling. Very cool and comfortable to wear, it is usually found in plain or jacquard weaves and sometimes in knits.

**Challis.** A soft, crinkly textured, lightweight fabric, it's great for dresses and flowing skirts. Often made from rayon, challis is also found in wool and various blends. It's not the easiest to work with because of its light and airy texture, but it's very forgiving of sewing flaws.

**Dotted swiss.** A lightweight, plain-weave cotton fabric that has small dots woven into the fabric at regular intervals. Swiss cotton is very smooth and soft between the dots, and one of the more expensive cottons. Imitation dotted swiss is often a poly-cotton blend, in which the dots are either flocked or embroidered. It is much less expensive than the real thing, and usually is offered in more colors.

**Eyelet.** Usually cotton, but often a cotton-poly blend, this medium- to lightweight fabric has been embroidered with a series of eyelets, and usually small flowers or vines. Cheaper eyelets are usually solid fabric, and some are even printed, not embroidered. The circles within the eyelets are usually cut out, or removed chemically, so the fabric is light and airy. Easy to work with, but depending on the size of the holes in the individual eyelets, the finished dress may need something underneath it.

**Gauze.** Usually made in cotton or a poly blend, it is also available in wool (very nice) and silk (heavenly—if you can find it!). This very lightweight, crinkly textured weave can be tricky to handle because of its airiness, but the cotton and wool varieties are not as difficult to work with.

**Lawn.** Lawn is a very lightweight, plain-weave fabric that is heavier than voile but lighter than batiste. Usually cotton, though it is often blended, it is fairly easy to handle and presses very nicely.

**Seersucker.** A fun, airy, summer weave, seersucker is often woven with narrow stripes that alternate between smooth and puckered. It's also available in solids and plaids. This fabric is usually cotton, but can often be found in poly, poly blends, and silk (which is more difficult to work with). Most are light to medium in weight and perfect for shirts, shorts, suits, skirts, and dresses.

**Chambray.** A medium-weight plain weave, chambray usually is characterized by the warp threads being colored, while the weft threads are white. Most often seen in blue, it resembles lightweight denim, but it is also available in many colors. Once washed, chambray has a soft but substantial hand and is quite easy to sew.

**Quilting-weight fabric.** A medium- to lightweight plain-weave fabric, quilting fabrics are very durable, and lend themselves well to skirts, tops, and dresses. Good-quality quilting fabrics are more expensive than the standard weight you'll find at a large chain store, but they are worth it.

Ponte knit

Woven plaid suiting

(continued from page 15)

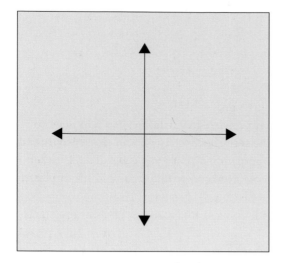

Lengthwise grain (warp)

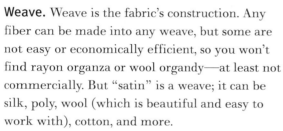

Crosswise grain (weft)

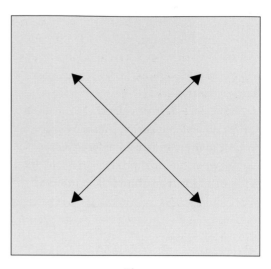

Bias

**Weave.** Weave is the fabric's construction. Any fiber can be made into any weave, but some are not easy or economically efficient, so you won't find rayon organza or wool organdy—at least not commercially. But "satin" is a weave; it can be silk, poly, wool (which is beautiful and easy to work with), cotton, and more.

Woven fabrics are made up of interlaced threads running lengthwise (also known as *straight of grain* or *warp*) and crosswise (also known as *weft*) that run from selvage to selvage. They usually only stretch in a diagonal (also known as *bias*) direction but can be stretchy in other directions if they contain spandex. Woven fabrics with a bit of spandex are wonderful for tailored dresses. The fabric retains the ability to hold its shape, allowing a little bit of give for comfort and a closer fit. In general, woven fabrics with a higher thread count—that is, more lengthwise and crosswise threads per square inch—are higher quality and tend to be easier to sew with as the threads don't warp as much and are more stable.

Knitted fabrics are made by looping and interlocking continuing lengths of yarn, and they stretch as a result of this construction. They require special treatment and equipment when sewing. (See Serger, page 13.)

**Texture.** Fabric can be smooth like voile, nubby as with dupioni silk, rough like wool, or only slightly textured like crepe. These qualities will all have an impact on the aesthetic quality of your final dress and how easy it is to sew. Shiny fabrics tend to be a bit more difficult to sew because they're slippery, so novice dressmakers should look for fabrics with a more stable surface.

**Drape, body, and weight.** How does the fabric fall? Is it soft and languid like a satin that will skim the body? Or is it stiff with more body like a cotton twill? Soft, drapey fabrics are wonderful for creating feminine silhouettes, which is why they're great for evening wear. For a more constructed, tailored look for the office, go with a fabric that holds its shape better.

Weight is also important to consider for drape and for warmth. Is the fabric heavy and thick like velvet and brocade, or is it light and thin like silk and cotton voile? Heavier fabrics tend to have less drape; lighter fabrics tend to have more.

## PREPARING FABRICS FOR SEWING

So, you've chosen your perfect fabric for your perfect dress; time to start sewing, right? Not so fast. Cleaning fabrics—either in the machine, by hand, or at the dry cleaners—tends to change the fabric a bit. Fabric can shrink, or cleaning can affect its feel and sheen, therefore it's important to prepare fabrics before you sew so you know what the final product will look like. A good general rule of thumb is to pretreat fabrics in the same way you will clean them after wearing. This also means that the garment has to be pretreated with all of its components in mind, so if the dress is to be made with interfacings, bonings, padding, and so on, those fabrics must be pretreated appropriately as well. Press fabrics that are wrinkled and can be safely pressed before sewing. You won't be able to cut the fabric accurately from the pattern unless it is really wrinkle-free.

If your fabric can be machine-washed and machine-dried, clean them this way before sewing. If the fabric is a knit, or has Lycra, wash and dry it at least two times—if not three—to make sure it has shrunk as much as possible. All too often, a finished garment continues to shrink a bit more in even the next washing. Shrinkage will almost always occur more with natural fibers than it will with synthetics. All cotton fabrics shrink, so preshrinking the fabric before sewing it up into a dress is important. To be extra safe, wash and machine-dry cottons twice, as they can shrink a bit more on the second washing. Hand-wash and line-dry delicate fabrics before sewing.

Wool and linen fabrics shrink a lot, and although dry cleaning should not cause shrinkage of these fabrics, it definitely does happen. To be safe, have wool and linen fabric lightly steam-pressed at the dry cleaner before sewing.

While you're pressing your fabric, also check to see that it's on grain. Pull the corners if needed, then press it flat so it will stay *on grain* (see Trueing, following section). Some low-quality fabrics will be badly off grain, and you'll never be able to straighten them or get a finished garment to hang right. Another reason to not buy low-quality fabric!

## TRUEING FABRIC

After preparing your fabric, you will need to make sure the lengthwise and crosswise threads are perpendicular to each other. This is called *trueing* or *blocking* the fabric, and it's important to do so that the final garment and its seams will be stable, smooth, balanced, and symmetrical. Have you ever cut a piece of fabric and noticed that, even though you cut it straight, the corners are not at right angles? This is because the fabric is *off grain* and needs to be blocked. It's easy to do. First, make sure the fabric is cut exactly along the crosswise grain (from selvage to selvage). You can do this by making a small cut and then ripping the rest of the fabric across

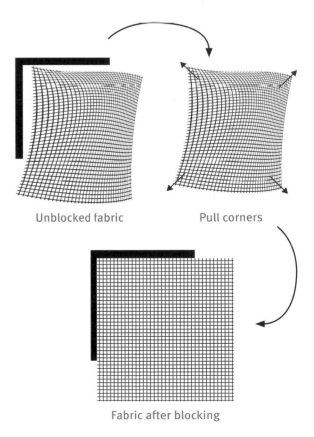

Unblocked fabric          Pull corners

Fabric after blocking

the width. I don't recommend this for good fabric (but I do it with muslin) because you can damage 2"–3" (5cm–7.5cm) of fabric near the torn edge.

If you don't have enough fabric to risk the loss of 2"–3" (5cm–7.5cm), you can do this instead. Find a single crosswise thread and pick it out with a pin. Then pull the thread out. This will give you a line on which to cut. Repeat on both ends (from selvage to selvage) of your yardage. Next, check all the corners against a right angle. A T square, L square, or even a piece of paper will work for this. If they're not square, simply pull the fabric diagonally (on the bias) in both directions. Check the corners again against a right angle. Continue blocking until all corners are perfect right angles. Press the fabric to keep it true.

## DRESSMAKING BASICS

### TYPES OF STITCHES

You really only need a few basic stitches—mostly on a sewing machine—to make the dresses in this book. There are lots of useful, even beautiful hand stitches, but you don't need many for the projects in this book.

#### MACHINE STITCHES
Straight stitch. This is the essential stitch that you'll use for almost all stitching.

Zigzag. You can use this stitch to finish the raw edge of a seam allowance to prevent it from fraying. Or use a narrow zigzag stitch to sew knits, as the zigzag stitch will stretch with the fabric.

Overlock stitch (optional). Some sewing machines come with this stitch, which resembles the stitch of a serger sewing machine and requires a special presser foot. It finishes the raw edge of a seam by wrapping thread around the edge, preventing it from fraying. The overlock stitch uses a lot of thread, is slow to use, and can

be a bit bulky, but if you have a fabric that is particularly prone to fraying, it comes in handy.

Serger stitch (optional). You need a special serger sewing machine for this stretchy stitch that is used to sew knits. It is also used to finish the raw edges of seam allowances by covering them in thread. Look at the seam allowances of almost any manufactured garment and you'll see serger stitches.

Staystitching. Staystitching is done to stabilize a curve, like a neckline or armhole, in a garment to prevent it from stretching out of shape. When fabric is cut in a curved shape, it can potentially stretch because any curve necessitates cutting the fabric on the bias. You can staystitch the curved openings of your fabric after you cut it out. Use a short stitch length and sew ⅛" (3mm) away from the stitching line, toward the seam-allowance raw edge. This will ensure that the staystitching is hidden in the seam when the garment is assembled.

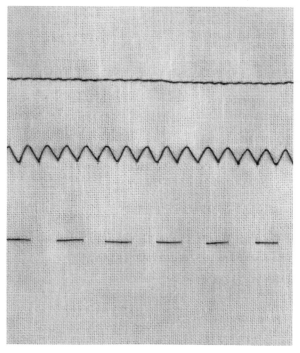

From the top: a straight stitch, zigzag stitch, and a basting stitch

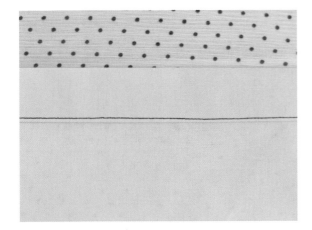

A machine-hemmed skirt

**Machine hemming.** All or most non-circle skirt patterns in this book are made with a built-in ⅜" (1.5cm) hem allowance. Narrow hems are good to use on very lightweight fabrics like chiffon. To make a narrow ⅝" (1.5cm) hem, fold and press the raw edge of the bottom of the garment to the wrong side by ¼" (6mm). Fold and press again by ⅜" (1cm). Stitch close to the folded edge. The finished hem will measure ⅜" (1cm). You can add a bit to the pattern hem for a wider hem, which is typically used for fabrics with more body and stiffness. To make a wider hem, add the desired amount to the ⅝" (1.5cm) seam allowance. For a finished hem that measures 1" (2.5cm), add 1" (2.5cm) to the pattern hem. Fold and press the hem to the inside first by ⅝" (1.5cm) and again by 1" (2.5cm). Stitch close to the folded edge.

**Narrow hem for a circle skirt.** It's difficult to sew a neat hem on a circle skirt by machine unless it is very narrow. This is because the raw edge of the folded-under hem will be wider than the fold. The bigger the hem, the more of a problem this becomes. Think about folding the wide edge of a cone under to visualize the concept. The solution is to sew a very narrow hem so that there is little difference between the edge and the fold. Fold the edge of the skirt to the inside by ¼" (6mm) and press. Stitch the hem ⅛" (3mm) from the fold. Trim the seam allowance close to the stitching. Fold over again by ¼" (6mm) and stitch close to the folded edge.

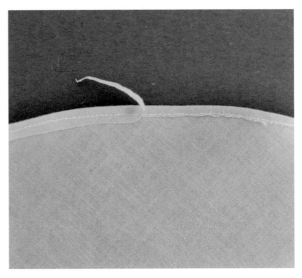

A circle skirt hem folded once and trimmed

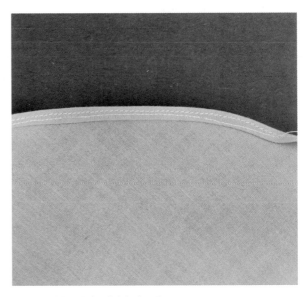

A circle skirt hem folded twice

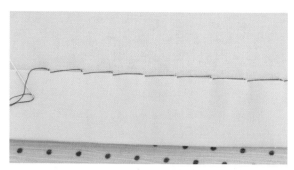

A blind hem stitch in progress on the inside of a garment

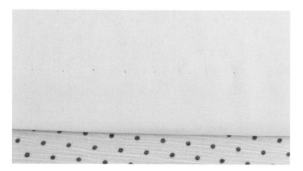

A finished blind hem stitch on the outside of the garment

## HAND STITCHES

Basting stitch. A basting stitch is a long, straight, easy-to-remove running stitch that is used to temporarily hold two pieces of fabric together.

Blind hem stitch. This stitch is used for hemming finely tailored suits and dresses. It's also great for sewing circular hems like on a circle skirt where machine-hemming is difficult. This stitch is barely visible on the outside of the garment. Begin by taking the first stitch in the fold of the hem. Then pick up just one or two threads from the skirt with your needle. Moving from right to left, pass the needle through the hem fold again. Don't pull the threads too tight, just enough so that the hem lies flat against the skirt. Continue in this way until the hem is sewn.

## MAKING A MUSLIN

A muslin, also known as a *toile*, is a test garment made from inexpensive fabric. Unbleached cotton called muslin is used often for this step (hence the name), but a muslin doesn't need to be made from muslin fabric. Use any inexpensive fabric that is close in weight and drape to the fabric you intend to use for the finished dress.

This test garment allows you to make sure the sewing pattern works and the fit is good before cutting your more expensive fabric. If you find problems with the fit of the muslin, you can make alterations to the pattern (see page 189). After addressing any fitting concerns, it's best to make another muslin to ensure a proper fit before proceeding to using your more expensive fashion fabric.

Admittedly, making a muslin sounds like a time-consuming chore, but it is seriously well worth it. You really don't know how well a pattern will work and fit you until you actually sew something from it. Making a muslin takes more time up front, but in the end the process saves you from having to throw away the garment because it cannot be fixed.

The nice thing about a muslin is that it's fairly quick to make compared to an actual finished dress because there is no hemming, facing, or finishing of any kind required. You do have to put a zipper in to be sure it fits properly, but besides basting the seams, that's about it. Once you've perfected the pattern by testing a muslin, you never have to do it again. You can now use the same pattern over and over without having to make a muslin because you know the pattern works.

## PINNING

Some people feel more comfortable pinning before sewing, and that's fine, but pinning is not an absolute necessity. I rarely do it, and neither do professional sewers in the garment-manufacturing industry. This is because it's time-consuming and unnecessary. There are lots of things I do use pins for, such as attaching a set-in sleeve, hemming, and inserting a zipper. Pinning is also helpful when sewing bias areas that stretch, such as necklines and armholes. But for most of the assembly process, if you've cut the fabric carefully and accurately from the pattern, then simply lining the pieces up, using the notches transferred from the sewing pattern as a guide, and holding them together as you sew works just fine. Just make sure that your pieces continue to line up as you sew. That said, when you do pin, always pin perpendicular to your stitching line. This makes it much easier to remove the pins as you sew.

## FACING VERSUS LINING

A common dressmaking conundrum is whether to fully line a dress or whether to use facings instead. In both cases, the idea is to finish the edge of the dress openings (except the hem) in a neat and inconspicuous way. Both methods work well for this. For both facings and linings, you can use an inexpensive fabric that coordinates with your fashion fabric. You should also choose one that will not affect the drape of the fashion fabric.

Facings, when made correctly, have the advantage of also helping the garment openings—necklines and armholes especially— to keep their shape. Separate facings require

less fabric, making this option a bit more economical. And separate facings are a little more straightforward in terms of assembling the garment, making them a great option for beginners.

A lining is often (but not always) made exactly like the dress itself using the same pattern but a thinner lining fabric. This is then sewn to the inside of the dress. You may want to fully line a garment if the fashion fabric is scratchy or slightly see-through. Or you may want to line only the bodice to give it a bit more structure. Linings can be a little more complicated; a different procedure is called for if you're lining a dress with a back zipper, a side zipper, or sleeves. But linings give a nice finish to the inside of the dress by hiding all of the seam allowances.

## FACINGS

A facing is a mirror image of just a part of a pattern piece, like a neckline, armhole, or the top of a skirt. Making the facing slightly smaller than the corresponding fashion fabric helps to keep it from peeking out from inside the garment.

To make a facing for the armhole and/or neckline, trace the edges on both the front and back of the pattern that you want to face. Where

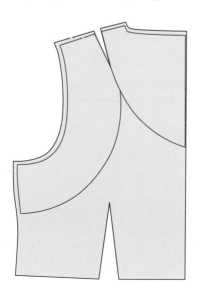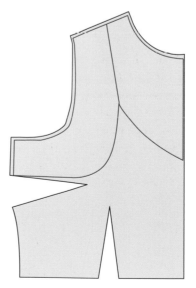

Tracing the facings for a standard bodice with shoulders

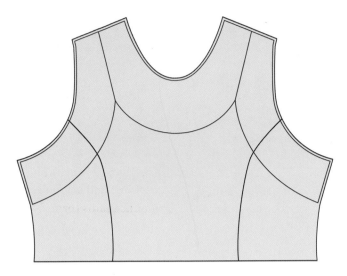

Tracing the facings from an assembled bodice

possible, make the facing at least 2" (5cm) wide plus the seam allowances. Make it even wider where possible, at the center front or center back, for example; a width of more than 2" (5cm) will help keep the facings from flopping out of the bodice. But you won't always be able to do this; at the shoulder of a bodice, for example, there won't be enough width to make both the neckline and armhole facings 2" (5cm) plus seam allowances without some overlap, which would cause bulk. As long as most of the rest of the facing is at least 2" (5cm) wide plus the seam allowances, it will work. Trace the pattern to within 1/16"–1/8" (1cm–3mm) of the edge. Cutting the facing this tiny bit smaller than the bodice will help the facing roll to the inside of the garment, making it less likely to peek out from under the fashion fabric.

When making a facing for a strapless bodice, you only need to include the side seams, not the front- or back-shaping seams. Because a facing is not long enough to pass over a curve, it doesn't need these shaping seams. For the same reason, facings don't generally include darts. To make the facing for a strapless bodice from the pattern pieces, overlap the center front and side front pieces at the notches that indicate the 5/8" (1.5cm)

seam allowance. Do the same with the center back and side back pieces. The pieces will overlap by 1¼" (3cm). This way you are tracing the pattern as it will be when it is sewn; if you don't exclude the shaping seam allowances, the facing will be too big. Trace the top edge of the bodice, making the facing at least 2⅝" (7cm) wide. Trace to within 1/16"–1/8" (1cm–3mm) of the top and side edges of the pattern to ensure the finished facing will roll to the inside of the bodice.

You can also trace an already assembled (sewn) part of the garment to make the facing. This ensures your facing will not include the shaping seams or darts. Press the assembled piece that you're tracing very well first.

Facings are assembled in the same way as the garment—that is, sewn at the shoulder and side seams with right sides together. After the facings are assembled, they are sewn to the opening being faced with right sides together. If the facing is sewn to a curved area, like a neckline or armhole, the seam allowances are then graded (page 35) and clipped (page 36). The facing is then turned to the inside of the garment and pressed. Understitching (page 36) the facing to the bodice seam allowance prevents it from peeking out of the bodice.

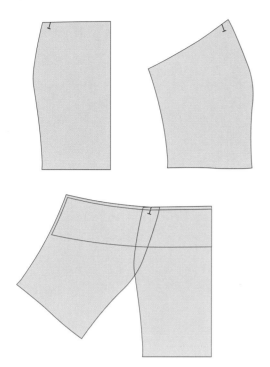

## LININGS

Most often a lining is made exactly the same way as the dress. Sometimes, though, a lining is made differently than the dress to cut down on bulk. For example, on the Grecian Goddess Dress (page 52), the lining is not gathered in order to make the finished garment less bulky. The outer silhouette of the lining and dress are the same shape so they can be sewn together without a problem.

Lining a strapless dress (page 73) or one that doesn't have a shoulder seam, such as a halter that ties around the neck (page 77), is pretty straightforward. The assembly procedure is the same as when facing these types of garments.

When working with a dress that is sewn front to back with a shoulder seam, the order in which a garment is assembled is a bit different when it is lined than when it is faced. Lining dresses with a back zipper, side zipper, or sleeves all require a different procedure.

### *Assembling a lined sleeveless bodice with a back zipper*

**1.** Sew the front and back bodice darts or seams if you're working with the princess bodice (page 98). Sew the fashion-fabric front and back bodice pieces with right sides together at the shoulders only. Repeat with the lining. With right sides together, sew the lining to the bodice at the neckline and armholes, but not the side seams. Grade the seams (page 35) and clip the curves (page 36).

**2.** Pull the bodice right side out through the shoulders.

**3.** Arrange the bodice so that the side seams of the fashion fabric are right sides together and the side seams of the lining are right sides together. Sew in this position. Leave the back seam open for the zipper. See page 32 for how to add the skirt.

*Assembling a lined sleeveless bodice with side zipper*

**1.** Sew the front and back bodice darts (or the seams if you're working with the princess bodice, page 98) of the fashion fabric and lining. Sew the fashion-fabric front and back bodice pieces with right sides together at the shoulder and one side seam. Repeat with the lining fabric. With right sides together, sew the lining bodice to the fashion-fabric bodice around the neckline. Grade the neckline seams (page 35) and clip the curve (page 36).

**2.** Turn the lining to the inside of the bodice through the neckline. Fold the fashion fabric up so that you're looking at the wrong side of the lining and the wrong side of the fashion fabric. Grasp the seam allowances of the fashion fabric and lining under the armhole at the top of the side seam. Place the seam allowances so that they are right sides together and pin.

*Assembling a lined bodice with sleeves and side zipper*

**1.** Sew the fashion-fabric front and back bodice darts (or the seams if you're working with the princess bodice, page 98). Repeat with the lining. Sew the fashion-fabric front and back bodice pieces with right sides together at the shoulders and one side seam. On the other side seam, sew only the top 2" (5cm) under the armhole. Leave the rest of the seam open for the zipper. Repeat with the lining. Sew the sleeves to the fashion fabric bodice (page 134). With right sides together, sew the lining bodice to the fashion-fabric bodice at the neckline. Grade the seams (page 35) and clip the curve (page 36).

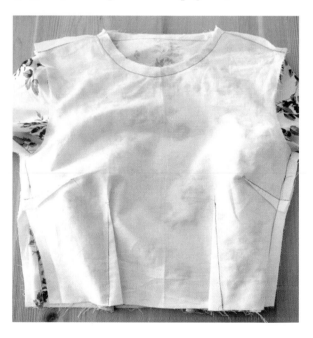

**3.** Sew the lining to the bodice with right sides together around the armhole. This is a bit awkward, so take your time and make sure you are sewing the armhole seam allowances only and not stitching through any other part of the bodice. Grade the armhole seams (page 35) and clip the curve (page 36). Repeat with the other armhole. Leave the side seam open for the zipper. See page 32 for how to add the skirt.

**2.** Turn the lining to the inside of the bodice through the neckline. Turn the bodice inside out so that the lining is on the outside. Sew the seam allowance of the lining armhole to the seam

allowance of the fashion-fabric bodice armhole. See page 32 for how to add the skirt.

## Assembling a lined bodice with sleeves and back zipper

**1.** Sew the fashion-fabric front and back bodice darts (or the seams if you're working with the princess bodice, page 98). Repeat with the lining

fabric. With right sides together, sew the fashion-fabric front to the back at the shoulders and side seams. Leave the back open for the zipper. Repeat with lining fabric. Sew the sleeves to the fashion fabric bodice (page 134). With right sides together, sew the lining bodice to the fashion-fabric bodice at the neckline. Grade the seams (page 35) and clip the curve (page 36).

**2.** Turn the lining to the inside of the bodice through the neckline. Turn the bodice inside out so that the lining is on the outside. Sew the sleeve allowances of the lining armhole to the sleeve allowances of the fashion-fabric bodice armhole. See page 32 for how to add the skirt.

## Adding the skirt to a lined bodice

If you're only lining the bodice but not the skirt, sew the finished skirt to both the fashion-fabric bodice and lining at the same time. If you're lining both the skirt and bodice, first sew the fashion-fabric skirt to the fashion-fabric bodice, then sew the lining skirt to the lining bodice. See page 32 for how to sew the skirt to the bodice.

## INTERFACING

Interfacing may seem like an unnecessary step, but it really helps a garment look finished and well made. Interfacing is used to give stability and structure to certain parts of a garment that need it, especially collars and cuffs. Used along a neckline facing, it prevents the neckline from losing its shape. On the back of a halter, interfacing prevents fabric from stretching, which will help it stay up without the support of a strap. When interfacing is used while inserting a zipper, it prevents the zipper from getting wavy, thereby distorting the silhouette of the garment. When used on a facing, interfacing is cut exactly the same as the facing and applied to the wrong side of the fabric. Interfacing comes in light, medium, and heavy weights, woven and nonwoven, and fusible or nonfusible (sew-in). You'll use light or medium weight most often for dressmaking, but always match interfacing weight to fabric weight.

Nonwoven fusible interfacing works great for most fashion fabrics. It is applied to the wrong side of the fabric, usually a facing, with an iron and damp cloth that activates the glue in the interfacing and bonds to the fabric. Follow the manufacturer's instructions for fusible interfacing; never iron directly on it, or the glue will stick to your iron.

Sew-in interfacing is pinned and then sewn along the edges to the wrong side of the fabric. Use a smaller seam allowance than what you'll use to assemble the garment when attaching sew-in interfacing so that the stitching will be hidden in the seam of the finished garment. After attaching the interfacing, trim the seam allowance of the interfacing to reduce bulk in the seam (see page 35 for more about seam grading).

Woven interfacing comes in both fusible and nonfusible. It is used with light or delicate fabrics because it is less likely than nonwoven interfacing to change the drape of the fabric.

Cut woven interfacing with the lengthwise and crosswise grains in the same direction as the fabric. If you don't, it could negatively affect the drape of the fabric.

Interfacing can be used with both facings and linings. It is easier to use interfacing with a facing than with a lining, however, because you can use the same pattern as the facing to cut the interfacing pieces. With a lining you would have to make a pattern for the interfacing (in the same way you would for a facing, see page 25) creating an extra step. In both cases the interfacing is applied to the wrong side of the facing or lining according to the manufacturer's instructions.

That said, it's not essential to use interfacing, I've made many dresses, especially less formal dresses like a sun dress, without interfacing that hold up just fine. And lots of ready-to-wear garments don't include interfacing. But interfacing can help a garment to keep its shape. As with many things in dressmaking, the fabric choice, the dress design, the look you're after, and how much wear and tear you want the final garment to stand up to will affect whether or not to use interfacing.

## UNDERLINING

Underlining is often used with very light or sheer fabrics to lend them a bit more structure or to prevent them from being see-through. You might use underlining with lace, for example, as in the Simply Chic Dress (page 169) Underlining can be used with any weight fabric: For instance, a medium-weight fabric for a strapless bodice could use more structure, so an underlining would be perfect for the bodice, even though you might not want to use it in the skirt.

The underlining is cut from the same pattern pieces as the main fabric. It is then pinned to the wrong side of the main fabric, and the two fabrics are then basted together by hand ¼" (6mm) from the edge. The pieces are also basted together along the dart markings. The fabric and the underlining are then treated as one fabric when assembling the garment. The basting stitches are removed after the garment is assembled. When underlining is used, a facing or a lining is generally required, as an underlining does nothing to finish or cover the raw seam allowances.

## BONING

Boning can give a bodice, especially a strapless bodice, more structure so that it will stay up without straps. There are many different kinds of boning used for dress and corset making. For the dresses in this book the lightweight flexible kind called Rigilene will work fine. It comes in ¼" (6mm) or ½" (13mm) widths; either is fine. It is sewn directly to the vertical seam allowances of the sewn lining or underlining, or, if you're not using a lining, to the seam allowances of the bodice. Cut the boning to the length of the seam minus ⅛"–¼" (3mm–6mm) to prevent the boning from poking out at the top and bottom edges of the bodice. Trim the ends of the boning into a curved shape to prevent the sharp edges from poking you, and sew a tiny piece of scrap fabric to the ends to prevent the ends from scratching you. Place the Rigilene on the pressed open seam allowance. Stitch down one seam allowance, then the other, sewing it to the seam allowance only, not through to the front of the fashion fabric.

## ATTACHING THE SKIRT

Whether you've designed your dress for a side zipper or a back zipper, the process for sewing the skirt to the bodice is the same. Make sure all seams are pressed open and the darts are pressed toward the center front and center back. Arrange your skirt inside out. Place the bodice inside the skirt, right sides together, with the raw edges of the waistlines aligned. Align the side seams and darts (where applicable). Stitch around the waistline.

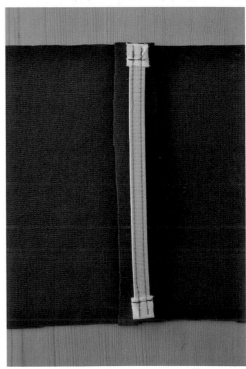

Sewing a length of Rigilene into a seam allowance

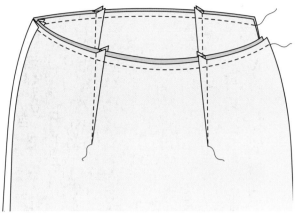
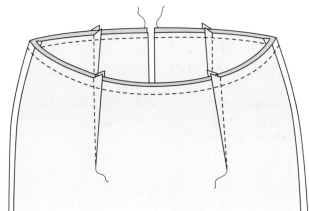

From left to right: a side zipper and back zipper

## ZIPPERS

Installing a zipper is really not hard. It takes just a bit of patience and precision. Invisible zippers are the best option for all of the projects in this book as they are barely visible—except for the zipper pull—from the outside of the garment, and they mimic the look of modern ready-to-wear clothing.

An invisible-zipper presser foot is very helpful. If you don't have one, you can buy a universal invisible-zipper foot that works with most machines anywhere invisible zippers are sold. These plastic feet can be used successfully to install an invisible zipper, but a metal foot that works specifically with your machine is the best option. If your machine didn't come with a metal invisible-zipper foot, you can often find one that's compatible with your machine online. You can also use a regular zipper foot in a pinch; it doesn't allow you to get really close to the zipper teeth as easily as you could with an invisible-zipper presser foot, but it can be used effectively to install an invisible zipper. I know a few expert seamstresses who use a regular zipper foot for all types of zippers.

Prepare by opening the invisible zipper and pressing it with your iron on the synthetic setting. The zipper teeth will be curled up a bit initially. Press the zipper as flat as you can get it

so that you can see the stitching that runs next to the zipper teeth. The seam you're sewing it to should be unsewn. Make sure that the lining or facing is pressed to the inside of the garment. Baste the facing or lining to the fashion fabric along both sides of the open seam ¼" (6mm) from the raw edge. Finish the seam allowances if desired (page 36).

*Installing a zipper*

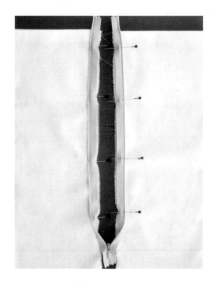

**1.** Pin the open zipper to the right side of the fabric along both seam allowances as shown. Align the top of the zipper where the teeth end with the top of the open seam. Align the zipper teeth with the ⅝" (1.5cm) seam allowance stitching line (you can mark this beforehand with tailor's chalk or by pressing a crease with your iron, if you desire) on both sides of the seam.

**2.** Sew the zipper to both seam allowances in this position.

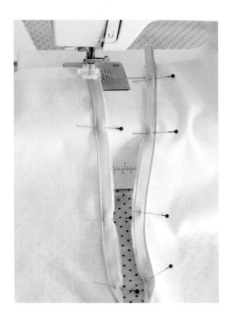

**3.** Fold the zipper tapes over the top edge and tack (sew a couple of stitches in the same place to secure) in place by hand or machine.

**4.** Fold the seam allowances to the inside of the garment and tack in place at the top of the zipper through the zipper tapes. To finish sewing the rest of the seam, switch to a regular presser foot. Pull the bottom of the zipper out of the way and stitch.

A zipped-up invisible zipper

## BUTTONHOLES

Sewing a buttonhole is not hard, but if you've never done it you'll want to practice on some scrap fabric first. To figure out the length of the buttonhole, measure the diameter of the button and its thickness. Add these measurements together plus ⅛" (3mm) and make a mark this length with tailor's chalk or a dressmaker's pencil on the fabric.

Many modern sewing machines come with a special buttonhole presser foot and an automatic one-step or a four-step buttonhole function. The procedure differs slightly depending on your machine, so if your machine has a buttonhole function, consult your machine's manual.

All machine-made buttonholes consist of the same elements, no matter how they are achieved: two parallel rows of narrow, tight stitching with bar tacks (reinforcement stitches sewn back and forth without the fabric moving) at both ends. The buttonhole is sewn continuously without cutting the threads until the end.

## Sewing buttonholes manually

**1.** Set your machine to the zigzag stitch. Set your stitch length to 0 and your stitch width to 5. You may need to try a few different width settings to achieve the right one for your machine and the fabric you're using. Make 5 or 6 bar tacks at one end of your button mark.

**2.** Lift the needle. Change the stitch length to 0.5 and the width to 2. Start with the needle at one end of the bar tack and sew down one side of your button mark.

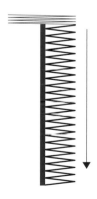

**3.** Lift your needle and set the length back to 0 and the width back to 5. Sew another 5 or 6 bar tacks.

**4.** With the needle down and presser foot up, turn the fabric 180 degrees. Set the length back to 0.5 and the width back to 2, and sew up the other side of the mark. Carefully cut open the fabric between the stitches with a seam ripper, taking care not to cut any of the stitching.

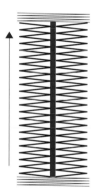

## GRADING, CLIPPING, AND UNDERSTITCHING

These three techniques are employed after the garment (or piece of a garment, such as a collar) has been sewn together and the facings or lining have been attached to the garment.

### GRADING THE SEAMS

Grading helps reduce bulk in a seam so that it won't be bumpy and will lie flat. When seams can be pressed open, as with a side seam, you don't need to grade the seams. You do need to grade the seams when two seam allowances are lying next to each other, as with a neckline facing where the seam allowance of the bodice neckline and the seam allowance of the facing are next to each other. It is achieved by trimming down one seam allowance, often to half the width of the other seam allowance.

### CLIPPING AND NOTCHING CURVES

To release the tension or reduce bulk and ensure a smooth curve, you will need to clip and notch the seam allowances of curved seams, like necklines and armholes, after they've been graded. A *clip* is a straight cut, while a *notch* is a little wedge shape that helps to reduce bulk. Clip inside curves, like a neckline; notch an outside curve, like the curved top edge of a sleeve. Either way, make sure not to cut through the line of stitching!

Graded and clipped seam allowances after turning and pressing

### UNDERSTITCHING

Understitching works wonders to prevent a facing or lining from peeking out from your dress. After you've sewn the facing to the bodice, grade the seams and clip the seam allowances, if you're working with a curve like a neckline. Press both dress and facing seam allowances toward the facing side of the seam. Then stitch both seam allowances, staying within ¼" (6mm) of the seam stitching, to the facing. As you stitch along the curve, keep the facing and seam allowances flat as they pass under your needle. The seam allowances will naturally splay out, which is the result you want.

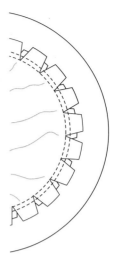

An understitched curve

### FINISHING THE SEAM ALLOWANCES

Ah, to finish or not finish the raw edges! Like many things in dressmaking, it depends on what works best for the design and the fabric. Finishing the seam allowances prevents fraying of the raw edges, and it also looks nice. But it's not always necessary. The seam allowance is usually finished either by stitching it with a zigzag or overlock stitch on a regular sewing machine or with a serger. The easiest way to finish a seam allowance is to simply cut it with pinking shears, which do a pretty good job of preventing fraying. Stitching the seam allowance works a bit better, unless you're working with very light, delicate fabric or something super slinky. In those cases, the bulk added to the edge of the seam allowance could make a bump that

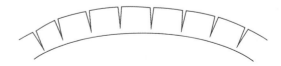

Single notched seam allowance

can show on the outside of the dress. For dresses that you plan to wash and dry in the machine a lot (such as those made of cotton), finishing the seams allowances will prevent the edges from fraying. For those dresses made of something you plan to dry clean, like wool, pinking the seam allowances should suffice.

## DRESS FORMS

If you plan to sew more than a few dresses, it's worth buying a dress form to help you fit your garments to your measurements. It's easier to see problems with the fit on the dress form than it is by trying the garment on and looking in the mirror.

There are many different kinds of dress forms, but choose one specially designed for sewing and fitting. Store-display forms typically don't come close to looking like an actual human body as they have odd, unrealistic proportions with large busts and tiny waists.

Dress forms are available as adjustable and nonadjustable types. Adjustable forms are great if you plan to sew for other people or if you tend to go up and down in size. They have dials at the neck, chest, waist, and shoulders that can be adjusted to a body's individual measurements. Nonadjustable forms are typically used in design schools. They have the advantage of being sturdier than adjustable forms, and they have seams down the front, back, sides, and around the waist that divide the body and serve as landmarks when designing or adjusting your own patterns.

No dress form can ever really accurately reflect an individual body. Even dress forms that are custom made from individual casts don't quite capture a body, because bodies move and their dimensions change just from breathing. Moreover, because everyone has a different body, a standard dress form that is made to reflect an "average" body will most often not duplicate an individual figure exactly. However, dress forms can still get you closer to the perfect fit.

There are very expensive forms that are made to a person's exact measurements or you can make an inexpensive dress form from duct tape or brown paper tape that is wrapped around the body. There are many DIY tutorials on the Web, though if, like me, the idea of being bound fairly tightly in duct tape makes you a bit nervous, you can buy a less expensive form slightly smaller than your personal dimensions and pad it out to the correct measurements. Using padding, you can much more accurately capture your own body's exact dimensions than with an adjustable form. An adjustable form allows you to alter only five parts of the body, whereas padding re-creates every curve and bump of your individual figure. A custom form becomes extremely helpful when making adjustments and alterations to a pattern.

From left to right: a store-display dress form, an adjustable form, and a nonadjustable form

# custom dress form

While there are companies that sell padding systems to fill out your form, you can do this yourself pretty easily and inexpensively using thin quilt batting and a stretchy body-shaping slip undergarment. I used a stretchy tube dress, which works if you only need to pad below the shoulders. If you need to pad the upper back or shoulders, you will need a garment that covers these areas as well. If you only need to pad the bust, you can just use a bra.

## SUPPLIES

Dress form slightly smaller than your measurements
Thin quilt batting
Stretchy body-shaping slip or bra

1.  Take your measurements according to the directions on page 40. Obviously it's really important to take them accurately in order to re-create your figure on the form. Take the dress form's measurements and compare. Note where you will need to add padding to reflect your own body and its curves and bumps. You can pad the form to your measurements, but it may not reflect your body accurately if the padding is not in the right place.

2.  Pad the form where necessary with long rectangles of batting and pin. For the bust, bottom, and hips, cut circles that graduate from larger to smaller to re-create the curve of these areas (see photo at right). Pad until the measurements are correct and the form looks like your figure. The main thing to keep in mind when padding is to proceed in thin layers to avoid bulkiness.

3.  Carefully pull the body shaper over the form.

# USING THE PATTERNS

## CHOOSING A PATTERN SIZE

The patterns at the back of the book run from size 1 through 12. Because sizing is not consistent in the clothing manufacturing industry, do not choose a size based on what you usually wear. Instead, take your measurements as follows, write them down, and pick your size according to the Size Chart (opposite page).

Wear the undergarments you would wear with a dress when you take these measurements. Use a soft tape measure. Make sure the tape measure is level all the way around and don't pull it too tight. Taking the following measurements accurately is important to achieving a good fit the first time.

**Bust.** Measure the fullest part of your bust all the way around your back.

**Waist.** Measure all the way around your waist at the smallest part.

**Hips or thighs.** Measure around the fullest part of your hips, making sure the tape measure passes over the fullest part of your backside. If your thighs are bigger than your hips, measure your thighs at the fullest part and use that instead of your hip measurement.

## CUTTING AND KEEPING

The patterns are overlapped on the pattern sheets and printed on both sides. You will need to trace the pattern you want to use in order not to cut through the other patterns. You can trace over them using large sheets of tracing paper; tape sheets of tracing paper together for the larger patterns. Or you can use a plastic see-through shower curtain and a very fine Sharpie marker to trace them. If you plan to use a pattern over and over again, I recommend tracing around the cut pattern onto oak tag or poster board so you have a sturdy, hard copy.

## DRESSMAKING TERMS USED IN THE BOOK

These are a few descriptions and instructions used in almost every project in the book or marked on the patterns themselves. It's helpful to become familiar with them before you begin.

### PATTERN MARKINGS

**Size.** This is indicated by color on the enclosed patterns: sizes 1 to 4 are black, 5 to 8 are gray, and 9 to 12 are light gray. Check the chart opposite to find your size.

**Seam allowances.** Most patterns included in the book use a ⅝" (1.5cm) seam allowance. This allowance is included on the pattern and is not marked—that is, the stitching line will be ⅝" (1.5cm) in from the cut fabric edges. It is important to keep this allowance in mind when making adjustments to the patterns.

**Stitching line.** The line you will actually sew is not marked on the patterns. For the collar and collar band patterns, it is located ⅜" (1cm) in from the edge of the pattern; for most other patterns, it is located ⅝" (1.5cm) in from the edge of the pattern. Some of the pattern modifications in the book will require that you draw in this line.

**Grain line.** The two-headed arrows indicate the direction in which to lay a pattern on the fabric. An arrow that runs up and down means that you lay the pattern on the fabric so that it aligns with the lengthwise grain (see page 20). An arrow

# size chart

| SIZE | BUST | WAIST | HIP |
|------|------|-------|-----|
| 1 | 32" (81cm) | 24" (61cm) | 34" (86cm) |
| 2 | 33" (84cm) | 25" (63.5cm) | 35" (89cm) |
| 3 | 34" (86cm) | 26" (66cm) | 36" (91cm) |
| 4 | 35" (89cm) | 27" (68.5cm) | 37" (94cm) |
| 5 | 36½" (92.5cm) | 28½" (72cm) | 38½" (98cm) |
| 6 | 38½" (98cm) | 30½" (77.5cm) | 40½" (103cm) |
| 7 | 40½" (103cm) | 32½" (82.5cm) | 42½" (108cm) |
| 8 | 42½" (108cm) | 34½" (87.5cm) | 44½" (113cm) |
| 9 | 44½" (113cm) | 36"½" (92.5cm) | 46½" (118cm) |
| 10 | 46½" (118cm) | 38½" (98cm) | 48½" (123cm) |
| 11 | 48½" (123cm) | 40½" (103cm) | 50½" (128.5cm) |
| 12 | 50½" (128.5cm) | 42½" (108cm) | 52½" (133.5cm) |

**note** *For the patterns in this book that align at the waist darts and side seams, it's best to pick the size for both the bodice and skirt that's closest to your waist measurement. Make alterations to the pattern (page 189), if necessary, to accommodate your bust and hip measurements.*

that runs diagonally across the pattern means you lay the pattern on the bias (see page 20).

**Center front, center back.** This indicates that the pattern is cut in half. Usually you will align the center front or center back of the pattern on the fold of fabric in order to cut a whole piece.

**Side front, side back.** The pattern is a whole piece and is *not* cut on the fabric fold.

**Darts.** These triangle-shaped wedges need to be transferred to the fabric so that you know precisely wear to sew the dart. One way to transfer the dart markings to the fabric with tailor's chalk or a dressmaker's pencil is to cut the dart out from the pattern and trace around it onto the fabric. Make sure you save the cut-out dart so you can use it to trace the bottom edge of the dart (the part that extends beyond the seam line). Whereas the rest of the pattern you're tracing is the cutting line, you're tracing the actual *stitching* line of the dart. So remember *not* to cut out the dart from your fabric.

**Notches.** On the patterns in this book, notches are the T-shaped markings along the seam lines. Notches located near a corner, such as the shoulder of the basic bodice, mark the ⅝" (1.5cm) seam allowance. Notches located somewhere in the middle of a seam, as on the curved part of the side front and center front strapless bodice patterns, show where to line up the pattern pieces that will be sewn together.

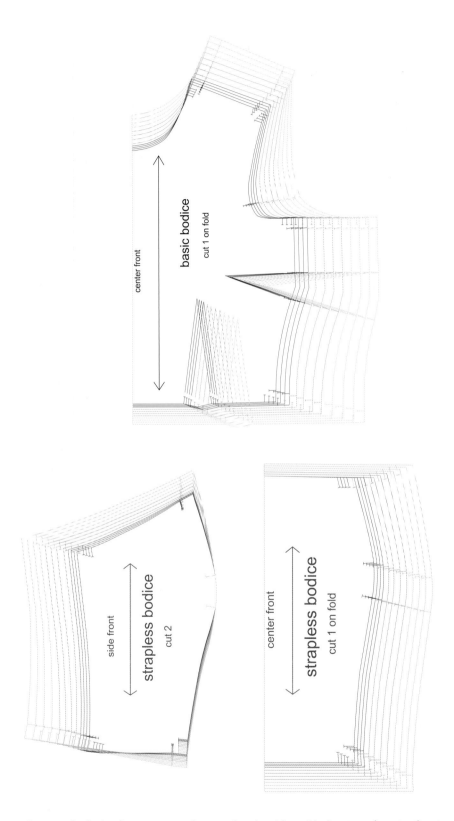

basic bodice
cut 1 on fold

center front

strapless bodice
cut 2

side front

strapless bodice
cut 1 on fold

center front

Counterclockwise from top: notches on the shoulder, side front, and center front

Transfer notches to the fabric using tailor's chalk or a dressmaker's pencil. You can also make small V-shaped cuts in the fabric seam allowance to indicate these notches. Make sure *not* to cut through the seam allowance.

### SEWING-SPECIFIC INSTRUCTIONS

**Press the seams open.** Open the seam allowances and press them flat with an iron. Pressing seams open with an iron after you sew them will make the inside of your garment neater and less bulky. Pressing the seams open is especially important when you're sewing one part of a garment to another. For example, when sewing the bodice to the skirt, there will be a lot less bulk in the side seams at the waist if the seams have been pressed open. Otherwise, you could end up with four seam allowances all sewn on the same side of a seam, causing too much bulk.

**Right side, wrong side.** *Right side* refers to the side of the fashion fabric that shows when the dress is worn; on a lining it refers to the side of the fabric you see when you look inside the dress. *Wrong side* is the other side of the fabric.

**With right sides together.** Sew the fabric with the right sides facing each other.

**Stitch close to the folded edge.** This refers to sewing an edge that has been folded under to the wrong side. Often it relates to a hem where you would sew about ⅛" (3mm) or less from the folded-under edge (not the bottom hem edge). See page 23 for an example.

**Baste.** Sew long stitches by hand or machine. Basting secures the fabric before permanent stitches are made. The stitches are often, though not always, later removed.

**Gather.** Sew 2 or 3 lines of basting stitches by hand or machine inside the seam allowance (closer to the raw edge) without backstitching. Gently gather, or pull, the fabric along the thread. The benefit of sewing multiple lines of stitches is that if one thread breaks you have one or two more to work with.

**Topstitch.** Sew on the right side of the fabric. This line of stitching will show on the outside of the garment.

## ASSEMBLING A DRESS

Each bodice pattern included in the envelope at the back of the book can be paired with any of the skirt patterns, plus many of the necklines, sleeves, and pattern-design options for hundreds of possible dress combinations. This is a good thing in terms of the huge number of options it provides. But, it's obviously not possible to include specific instructions for each and every one of these possible designs.

Each dress includes instructions for the specific pattern pieces used to create the sample, with illustrated steps for each of the separate bodice and skirt patterns. You'll find cross-referenced instructions for attaching the skirt to the bodice, inserting a zipper, using the neckline templates, and adding sleeves. When starting a project, it's best to review the Dressmaking Checklist below to ensure that you're following the necessary steps for your unique dress.

### DRESSMAKING CHECKLIST

#### 1. Plan Your Dress

☐ Choose the bodice and skirt styles you'll use to create your dress.

☐ If you will be modifying the neckline of your planned dress, pick one of the neckline templates.

☐ Choose a collar pattern (optional).

☐ Select a sleeve pattern (optional).

☐ Consider modifying the length of the skirt pattern you plan to use.

☐ Determine whether you will be lining the dress or facing it (see page 25 for more information).

☐ Opt for a back zipper or side zipper. *Note:* If you use the basic bodice (page 49) or princess bodice (page 98) and do not modify the neckline with one of the neckline templates to make it bigger, then you will need to make the bodice (and the skirt) with a back zipper. You won't be able to get your head through the unmodified neckline opening if you use a side zipper.

#### 2. Prepare the Patterns

☐ Take your measurements according to the instructions on page 40, write them down, and use them to pick the appropriate pattern size (page 41).

☐ Trace and cut your pattern pieces from the pattern sheets enclosed in the back of the book (envelope).

☐ Make alterations to the pattern to improve the fit, if needed (Chapter 6).

☐ Use a neckline template to modify the pattern (page 108), if desired.

☐ Modify the length of the skirt pattern, if desired (page 199).

☐ Add a ⅝" (1.5cm) seam allowance to the center back of the pattern (if it doesn't already have a back seam allowance, as with the bias skirt and straight skirts) if you prefer a back zipper instead of a side zipper. You will have to do this if you choose the basic or princess bodices as you will not be able to get your head through the neckline without a back zipper unless you modify the neckline to make it bigger.

#### 3. Prepare the Facing or Lining

☐ If you are facing the dress instead of lining it, use the bodice pattern to make the pattern for the facing (page 25).

☐ If you are lining the dress, see page 27. Lining the dress usually requires that the dress be sewn together in a different order than if you are facing the dress.

## 4. Make the Muslin

☐ Sew a muslin (page 24), using the prepared pattern pieces and the appropriate fabric-cutting layouts.

☐ Make alterations to the pattern (Chapter 6) as needed based on the fit of the muslin. To be safe, make another muslin.

## 5. Prepare the Fabric

☐ Launder, dry, and true the fabrics for the finished garment (page 21).

## 6. Make the Dress

☐ Cut your prepared fashion fabric, facing fabric, and interfacing or lining fabric based on the cutting layouts for your selected pattern pieces. See page 40 for how to use the patterns. Transfer markings for darts and notches (page 41) from the pattern using a dressmaker's pencil or tailor's chalk.

☐ Assemble and sew your chosen bodice from the fashion fabric. If using a collar, sew it on now. Line or face the bodice and add sleeves, if desired. Grade the seam allowances (page 35), clip all curves (page 36), finish seam allowances, if desired (page 36), and press.

☐ Assemble and sew your skirt from the fashion fabric, lining it if desired. Press and finish the seam allowances (page 36), if desired.

☐ Sew the skirt to the bodice (page 32).

☐ Insert the zipper in the dress (page 33).

## ADVICE FOR BEGINNERS

If you haven't sewn a lot of garments, it's best to start with something simple. Try the strapless (page 73) or basic bodice (page 49) with the straight skirt (page 169) for your first dress. Follow the directions as they are written without adding any of the sleeve or neckline options. Once you get a feel for the flow of the garment-assembly process, you can try changing the neckline, adding sleeves, or making the dress with a full lining.

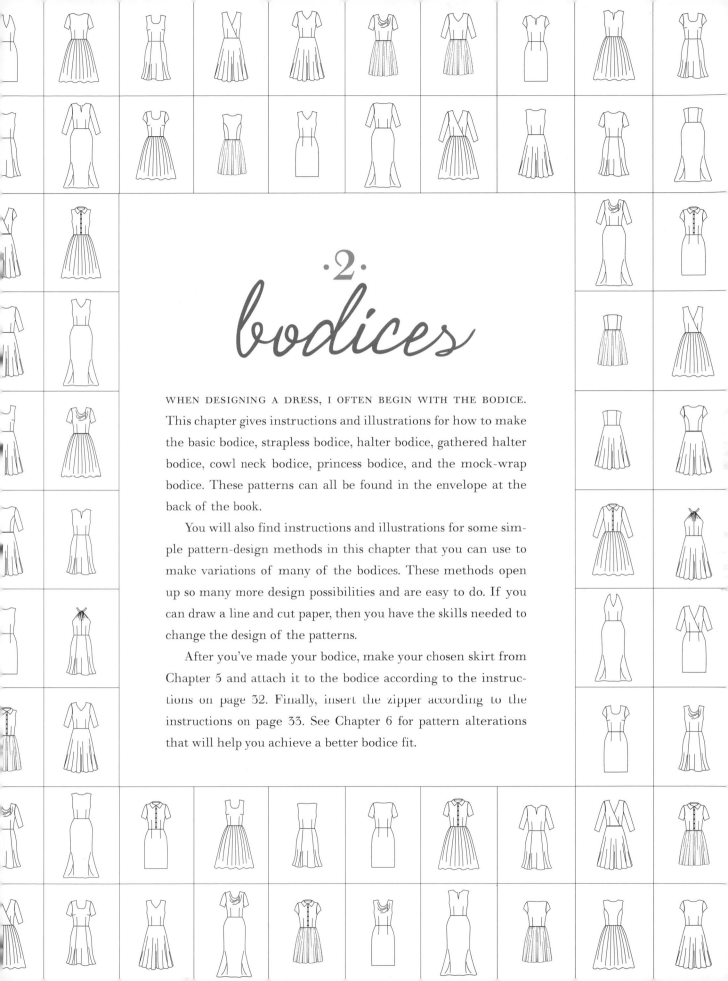

# ·2·
# bodices

WHEN DESIGNING A DRESS, I OFTEN BEGIN WITH THE BODICE. This chapter gives instructions and illustrations for how to make the basic bodice, strapless bodice, halter bodice, gathered halter bodice, cowl neck bodice, princess bodice, and the mock-wrap bodice. These patterns can all be found in the envelope at the back of the book.

You will also find instructions and illustrations for some simple pattern-design methods in this chapter that you can use to make variations of many of the bodices. These methods open up so many more design possibilities and are easy to do. If you can draw a line and cut paper, then you have the skills needed to change the design of the patterns.

After you've made your bodice, make your chosen skirt from Chapter 5 and attach it to the bodice according to the instructions on page 32. Finally, insert the zipper according to the instructions on page 33. See Chapter 6 for pattern alterations that will help you achieve a better bodice fit.

*day-to-evening sheath*
# THE BASIC BODICE

You will find countless design possibilities with this classic fitted bodice. Depending on the fabric and skirt style you choose, it is versatile enough to transition from day to night. Cover bare arms with a cardigan in the office, then switch out your flats for heels on your way out. These instructions are for sewing a basic bodice with a back zipper, facings, and no sleeves. The sample project pairs this bodice with the straight skirt (page 169).

## PATTERN PIECES

Front Basic Bodice (sheet 1 front)
Back Basic Bodice (sheet 1 front)

## YARDAGE

**FASHION FABRIC AND LINING FABRIC**
45" (114cm) fabric:
- Sizes 1 to 5: ¾ yard (68.5cm)
- Sizes 6 to 12: 1¼ yard (1.1m)

60" (152.5cm) fabric:
- Sizes 1 to 12: ¾ yard (68.5cm)

**TO FACE BODICE INSTEAD OF LINING, ADD**
½ yard (45.5cm) of 45" (114cm) or 60" (152.5cm) facing fabric
1 yard (0.9m) of 20" (51cm) interfacing

## SUPPLIES

Invisible zipper

**notes**
- *Use a ⅝" (1.5cm) seam allowance for all sewing.*
- *If you decide to add sleeves, then skip the armhole facings.*
- *If you will be lining the bodice, skip the neckline and armhole facings.*
- *The length of the zipper should be the length of the bodice's center-back seam or side seam (depending on where you plan to insert it) plus 8" (20.5cm).*

## FABRIC TIP

The basic bodice will work with a wide variety of fabrics from thin, lightweight, and drapey to heavier and stiffer. It all depends on the look you're after. See page 14 for more about fabrics.

## CUTTING LAYOUTS

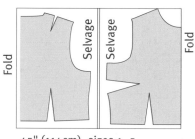

45" (114cm), sizes 1–5
60" (152.5cm), sizes 1–12

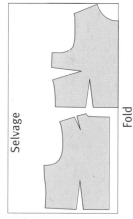

45" (114cm), sizes 6–12

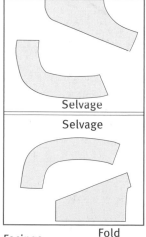

Facings

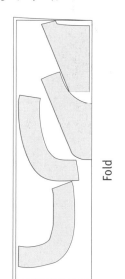

Interfacing

1. Trace and cut out the Front and Back Basic Bodice patterns from sheet 1. If you will not be altering the neckline to make it larger using the scoop, deep V-, or high V-neckline templates (Chapter 3), then you will need to add a ⅝" (1.5cm) seam allowance for a zipper to the back bodice pattern. If you do use a template or alter the pattern yourself to make the neck opening bigger, then you can add the seam allowance to the back bodice pattern for a back zip. Or use the pattern as is and insert a side zipper, cutting the back bodice pattern with the center back on the fold.

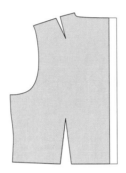

2. Trace the armhole and neckline of the front and back patterns to make the pattern for the bodice facings. Trace to within ¹⁄₁₆"–⅛" (1mm–3mm) of the edge. This will make the facings slightly smaller than the bodice, which will ensure that the facing rolls to the inside of garment and doesn't peek out. See page 25 for more about facings.

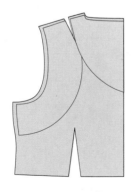

3. Cut the fashion fabric, facing fabric, and interfacing using the patterns according to the appropriate cutting layout for your fabric width and size. Sew the darts on the front and back bodice. Press the waist darts toward the center and the bust darts downward.

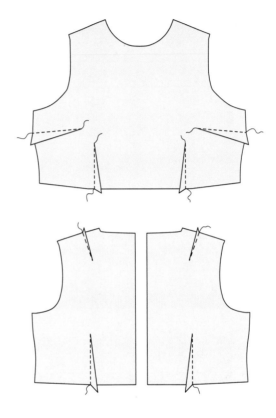

4. With right sides together, sew the front bodice to the back bodice at the shoulders and side seams. *Note:* If you are using a side zipper, leave one side seam open. Press the seams open.

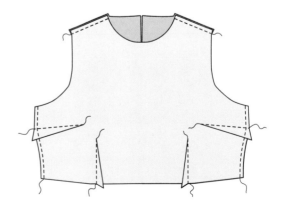

**5.** Apply interfacing to the wrong side of the facing pieces according to the manufacturer's instructions (see page 31 for more about interfacing).

**6.** Sew the armhole facings with right sides together at the shoulder and side seams. (Remember to skip this step if you are adding sleeves.) *Note:* If you are using a side zipper, leave the side seam of one of the facings open. Press all the seams open.

Sew the front neck facing to the back neck facing with right sides together at the shoulder. Press the seams open.

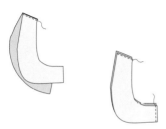

**7.** With right sides together, sew the neck and armhole facings to the bodice.

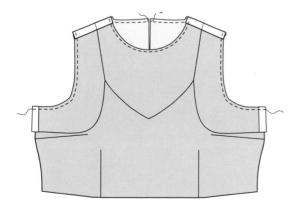

Grade all seam allowances, clip the curves, and understitch (see page 35) the armhole and neckline seam allowances to the facing. Finish the seam allowances (page 36), if desired. Press the facings to the inside of the bodice.

**8.** See page 134 for how to attach sleeves, if desired. See page 32 for how to attach the skirt to the bodice.

*grecian goddess dress*
# THE ONE-SHOULDER
# VARIATIONS

Who would ever guess that this skin-baring top evolved from the basic bodice?
Perfect for an evening affair, I think this would make a beautiful bridesmaid's
dress at a daytime wedding. It's paired here with the gathered A-line skirt
(page 178) that hits at the knee, but consider trying a floor-length skirt. I made
a one-shoulder bodice with gathers at the front shoulder, and also include an
option for a simpler design or darts shifted to the shoulder without gathers.

**notes**
- *Review basic dart manipulation techniques (page 60)
  before beginning this project. If you are familiar with
  moving darts around the bodice or turning darts into
  gathers, tucks, or fullness (page 60), the variations
  described here should be pretty straightforward.*
- *For the one-shoulder variations, use the same yardage
  amounts for your chosen pattern size and fabric width as
  the basic bodice (page 49).*
- *Instead of cutting out the patterns on the fold of fabric, cut
  them with fabric laid out flat in a single layer.*

**1. For a simple one-shoulder pattern:** Trace
and cut the Back Basic Bodice pattern from
sheet 1. Trace the pattern again to make a
complete back bodice pattern. Draw a line from
one shoulder to the underarm seam on the
other side. Cut out the new pattern.

Repeat the procedure with the Front Basic
Bodice pattern from sheet 1. Cut one from the
lining fabric and one from the fashion fabric
using the new patterns for both the front
and back.

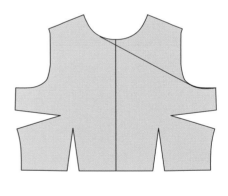

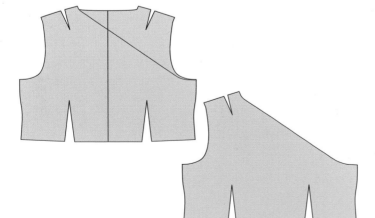

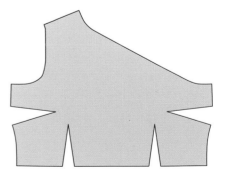

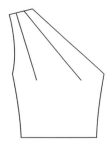

The finished front one-shoulder variation with darts shifted to the shoulder

**2. For a one-shoulder pattern with the darts shifted to the shoulder:** Trace and cut out the Front Basic Bodice pattern. Raise the bust points (page 60) and shift the bust dart to the waist (page 61). Trace the pattern again, turning it over and placing the two center-front edges together to make a complete front pattern and create the one-shoulder pattern by drawing a line from one underarm seam to the opposite shoulder and cutting along the line.

Draw a straight line from each of the bust dart tips to the shoulder. Slash the lines, shift the darts to the shoulder, and close the waist darts. You can shorten the darts so that they extend to about ½" (13mm) from the bust point, if desired (see page 60 for more about raising and lowering darts). Cut one from your fashion fabric and one from your lining fabric. Follow step 1 (page 52) to make the pattern for the one-shoulder back bodice.

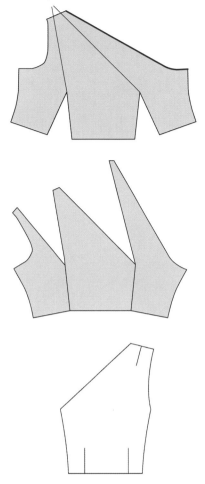

The finished back one-shoulder variation

**3. For a one-shoulder bodice with gathers at the front shoulder:** Follow step 2 but draw 3 lines from the tip of each bust point. Slash the lines, close the waist darts, and shift the darts to the shoulder, spreading the pieces evenly.

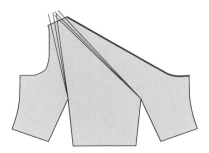

Trace the new shape to complete the pattern. Cut one from your fashion fabric using the new pattern. To make the patterns for the front and back lining pieces and the back bodice piece, follow step 1 on page 52.

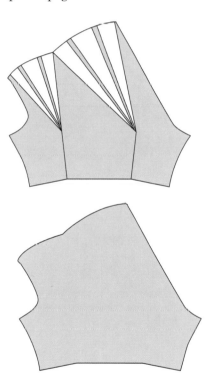

a. Sew a line of basting stitches along the top edge of the front fashion-fabric bodice piece.

Gather to the same size as the back bodice shoulder seam and sew the back fashion-fabric bodice darts. Press the darts toward the center.

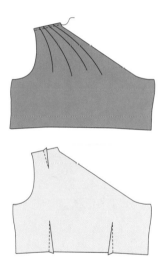

b. Sew the front bodice lining darts. Press bust darts downward and waist darts toward the center.

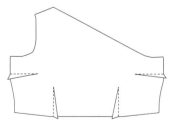

Sew the back bodice lining darts. Press darts toward the center.

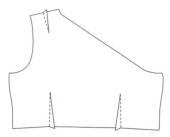

c. With right sides together, sew the front and back lining pieces together at the shoulder only. Press the seam open.

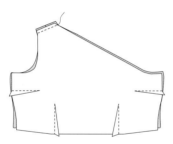

d. With right sides together, sew the front and back fashion-fabric pieces together at the shoulder only. Press the seam open.

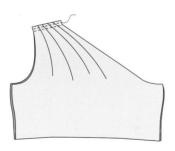

e. Open out the lining bodice and fashion-fabric bodice. With right sides together, sew along the armholes and neckline. Don't sew the side seams. Grade the seams (see page 35) and clip the curves (page 36).

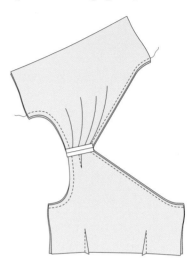

f. Turn the bodice right side out through the shoulder and arrange it in the position it will be worn.

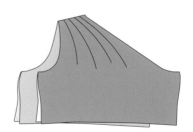

g. Fold the front and back fashion fabric up. The shoulder of the bodice will be sandwiched in between. Sew the lining at the side seams with right sides together. Sew the fashion fabric at the side seams with right sides together, making sure not to catch any other part of the bodice in the stitches.

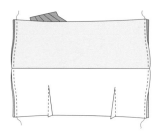

## *after midnight dress*
# THE SIMPLE YOKE VARIATION

Let's be honest: Who doesn't love to wear black? The trick to avoid looking too severe is all in the subtle details. In this youthful style, the sheer lace yoke fabric makes it more playful and sweet, especially when paired with a pleated skirt on the shorter side. The effect is similar to a strapless dress, but with all the practicality of a basic bodice.

A decorative yoke can create a very distinctive style statement when made with a contrasting fabric, especially when the fabric contrasts not only in color but in sheerness, like the dress shown. And it's super easy to do. Draw a curved line across the pattern from the side seam to the center front. The line should start ⅝" (1.5cm) under the armhole, then curve upward and over to the center front. You can use the Strapless Bodice pattern as a guide to draw the line, or you could draw a line from ⅝" (1.5cm) under the armhole straight across to the center front instead, but that technique is best reserved for color blocking with opaque fabrics. Otherwise, depending on your figure, the yoke could be pretty revealing. Because you slash all the way through the pattern creating a new seam line, you will need to add a seam allowance to both the new pattern pieces along the edges resulting from the slash: the bottom of the new yoke pattern piece and the top of the new bodice pattern piece.

# dart modifications

The basic bodice can be easily modified in lots of different ways. Moving darts around the bodice, dividing darts, and making darts into tucks or gathers is really easy and allows for so many design possibilities. If you can cut a piece of paper, you can do this! You can make these changes to most of the bodice patterns in the book but, if you're unfamiliar with the techniques, it's best to learn them first using the basic bodice (page 49).

First, a little bit about darts. You probably already know intuitively what darts do. If you've ever worn a fitted garment with darts versus a garment without darts, then you know that darts shape the fabric to the curves of the body. The shaping of the side seams of a skirt and the angled sides of a bodice are also darts of a sort, but they are darts hidden in a seam. Princess seams are another example of hidden darts. The main thing to remember about darts for the following bodice pattern variations is that a dart must begin at a seam and the pointy tip of the dart must be positioned at the highest point of the bust or bust point (basically at the nipple).

The basic bodice with darts at the bust and the waist

## RAISING DARTS

For aesthetic reasons, the tip of the darts on a bodice pattern are typically lowered ½" (13mm) or more from the actual highest point of the bust. To make changes to the darts we must first raise the darts so that the tip of the dart sits at the actual highest point of the bust curve.

**1.** To find the raised bust point (i.e., the actual high point of the bust) on a pattern with a bust and waist dart, draw a line through the center of each dart so that the two lines intersect and mark this point. Redraw the dart legs of both darts so that they extend to the higher point.

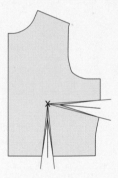

**2.** When you're done making changes to the pattern, lower the darts to their original position.

note *To find the raised bust point on a pattern with only one dart, such as a waist dart, you can use a two-dart pattern that you've already located the raised bust point on as discussed above. Just raise it the same amount as it was raised on the two-dart pattern.*

*Or, you can measure down from the intersection of your neck and shoulder to your bust point. You should wear the undergarments you plan to wear with a fitted bodice when you take this measurement. Mark this point on the pattern but be sure not to include the seam allowance when measuring down from the neck/shoulder intersection on the pattern. Starting from the bottom of the dart legs (the widest part of the dart), extend the darts to the bust point.*

## SHIFTING DARTS

**1.** To change the basic bodice pattern from a two-dart pattern to a one waist-dart pattern, start by tracing the Front Basic Bodice pattern from sheet 1, and then raise the darts as described on page 60. Cut out the new darts but leave a tiny hinge of paper at the bust point.

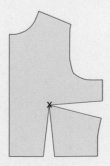

**2.** Rotate the hinged piece of the pattern upward until the side bust dart is closed, and tape it.

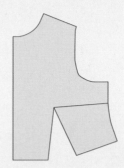

**3.** The waist dart will be bigger, but the shape of the bodice will be exactly the same when sewn. This is not necessarily intuitive, but to prove it, trace a copy of the original unmodified bodice pattern, cut out the darts, and then tape them together as they would be when they are sewn. Do the same thing with the new pattern and compare them. You'll see that when you superimpose one on the other, the shape is the same. The space that the darts occupy within the bodice has shifted around, but the amount of space taken up by the darts hasn't actually changed.

**4.** To finish the pattern, lower the bust point the same amount you raised it and redraw the dart legs to this point.

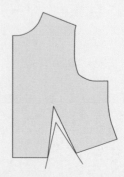

*Remember the seam allowances, and don't make the new dart too close to a seam allowance. For example, when shifting the dart to the side seam, make the new dart more than ⅛" (1.5cm)—maybe 1⅛" (4cm) to be sure—from the bottom of the armhole curve. If you were to make the dart ¼" (6mm) from the bottom of the armhole curve, the sewn dart would end up in the armhole curve seam allowance, making for a messy, bulky seam allowance that would be difficult to sew a sleeve to or finish properly. You can avoid confusion by marking and cutting off the ⅛" (1.5cm) seam allowance before you begin modifying the pattern. Remember to add it back on to the finished pattern.*

## SHIFTING DARTS TO THE ARMHOLES

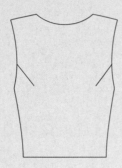

**1.** Begin with the single waist-dart pattern with raised darts described on page 61.

**2.** Draw a straight line from the tip of the dart to the armhole. Slash along this line, leaving a hinge.

**3.** Rotate the hinged piece downward until the waist dart is closed. Notice that the waistline now has a slight angle at the closed dart.

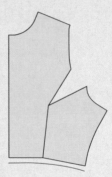

**4.** Trace the new pattern and smooth out the waistline angle with a subtle curve.

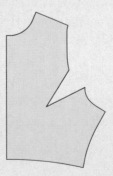

# SHIFTING DARTS TO THE SIDE SEAMS

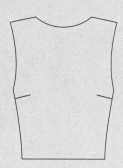

1. Begin with the single waist-dart pattern (page 61) and draw a line from the tip of the dart to the side seam at least ⅝" (1.5cm) below the underarm.

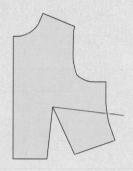

2. Slash the line and rotate the dart downward until the waist dart is closed.

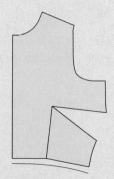

3. Trace the pattern, smoothing out the waistline angle with a subtle curve.

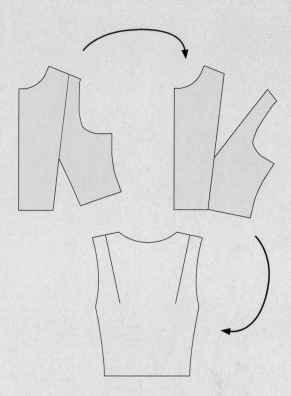

Use the same procedure as on page 62 to shift darts to the shoulder

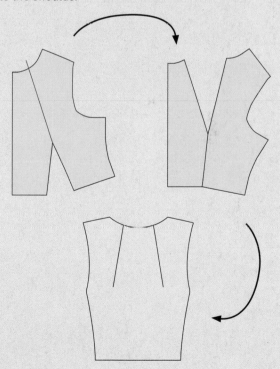

Use the same procedure to shift darts to the neckline

## SHIFTING DARTS TO CENTER FRONT

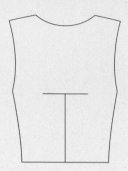

You can even shift the darts to the center front. Shifting the darts to the center front requires that the center front below the darts be made into a seam. Add a ⅝" (1.5cm) seam allowance to the seam below the darts to complete the pattern. This pattern piece would be cut with the perpendicular edge (from the neckline) of the center front pattern on the fold of fabric.

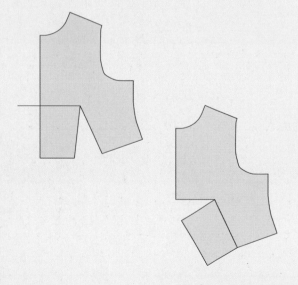

## CURVED DARTS

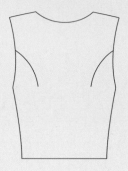

The new, shifted dart can even be curved! Use the same procedure as you would a straight dart.

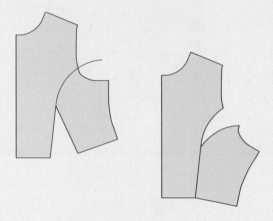

Actually, the dart could be a zigzag or any crazy shape. The shape of the dart legs will not affect the size of the new dart, though, of course, a zigzag-shaped dart would not be much fun to sew.

# THE EMPIRE WAIST VARIATION

You can also use dart shifting to change the pattern in other ways. For example, when creating the pattern for an empire waist bodice, you can shift the dart out of the way so that you can draw a line across the bodice without having to cross the open dart.

**1.** Start with the waist dart pattern (page 61) and draw a line from the dart tip to the armhole, leaving a hinge. Rotate the hinged piece downward and close the waist dart temporarily.

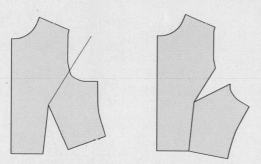

**2.** Measure from your waist to under your bust. Measure and mark the same distance from the pattern's waist stitching line. Draw a line across the pattern at this point.

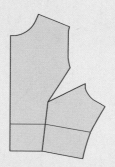

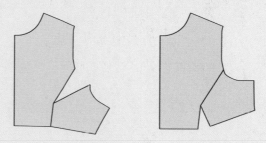

**3.** Slash the line and rotate the hinged piece upward to close the armhole dart.

**4.** Add a seam allowance to the bottom of the pattern where you slashed it.

Use the same process to make the changes to the back pattern. The empire waist bodice can easily be paired with a gathered skirt. Use the raised waist measurement of the empire bodice pattern to determine the waist measurement of the gathered skirt.

# DIVIDING A DART BETWEEN THE WAIST AND ARMHOLE

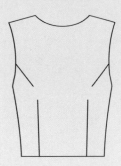

**1.** Begin with the pattern with the single waist dart (page 61).

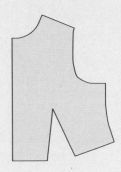

**2.** Slash the pattern to the armhole, leaving a hinge.

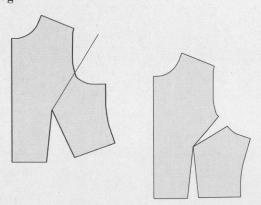

**3.** Rotate the hinged piece downward but don't close the waist dart completely.

# DIVIDING A DART THREE WAYS

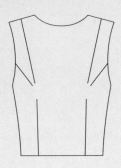

**1.** Slash the pattern to the armhole and shoulder, leaving hinges.

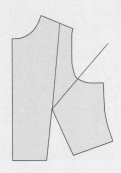

**2.** Rotate the hinged pieces downward, dividing the dart space equally.

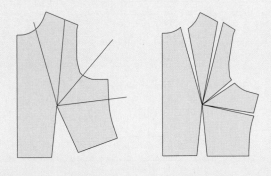

**3.** Add more slashes for more darts.

## DIVIDING A DART IN TWO AT THE NECKLINE

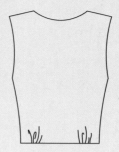

**1.** Draw 2 lines from the tip of the dart to the neckline.

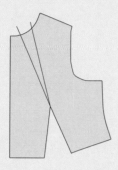

**2.** Slash, leaving a hinge, and rotate downward until the waist dart is closed, dividing the dart space at the neckline evenly.

## TURNING DARTS INTO GATHERS

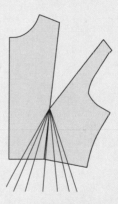

**1.** Start with the bodice pattern with the waist dart (page 61). Slash from the tip of the dart to the shoulder and shift the dart to the shoulder, closing the waist dart. Draw several lines from the dart point to the waistline. Draw the outside lines to make the dart about ¼" (6mm) larger than the original dart.

**2.** Slash the lines, leaving hinges, and then close the shoulder dart, spreading the pieces evenly. Trace the new shape and mark where the outside slash lines were with dots to indicate where to gather.

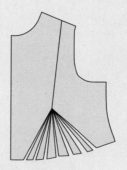
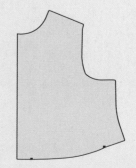

## UNFITTED BLOUSE CONVERSION

Follow steps 1 and 2 from Turning Darts to Gathers but skip the gathering marks. If desired, add some length to the bottom of the pattern. Make the same changes to the waist darts of the back bodice pattern and add the same length you did to the front bodice pattern. This pattern has the dart space necessary to accommodate curves, but the dart space is simply left unsewn.

## SEMIFITTED BLOUSE CONVERSION

You can also divide the unsewn dart space, shifting a little of it to a sewn dart making for a semifitted shirt.

**1.** Follow step 1 and 2 Turning Darts into Gathers (page 67). Then, on the front bodice pattern, slash a line to the side seam (not too close to the armhole seam allowance), leaving a hinge.

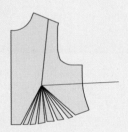

**2.** Open the side-seam dart a little. Add length as for the Unfitted Blouse if you won't be gathering it. Trace the new pattern. The new pattern can be gathered at the waist or left ungathered like the blouse in the photo.

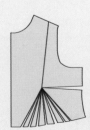 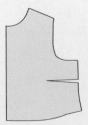

## GATHERED DARTS
## WITH A YOKE

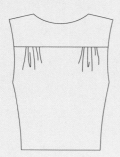

**1.** Start with the bodice pattern with the single waist dart (page 61). Align the waistlines of the front and back bodice patterns and draw a line across the top at the level where you want the yoke to be.

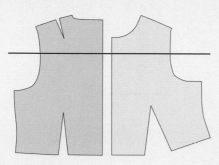

**2.** Slash the patterns along the yoke line. Draw lines from the tip of the dart to the yoke line. Slash the lines, leaving hinges. Close the waist dart and spread the slashed pieces for gathers.

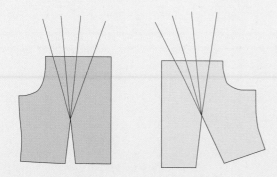

**3.** Trace the new pattern. Add ⅝" (1.5cm) seam allowances to the lower edge of the yoke and upper edge of the bodice where it was slashed.

## ADDING FULLNESS
## GATHERED AT THE WAIST

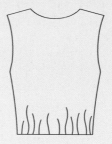

**1.** Start with the pattern with the ungathered dart (page 67). Draw straight, evenly spaced parallel lines through the pattern.

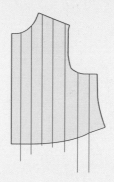

**2.** Slash the pattern, leaving hinges along the neckline, shoulder, and armhole. Spread evenly. The more you spread the more fullness will be created. Shift the center front of the pattern half of the spread between the other pieces.

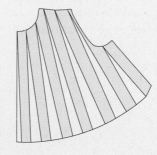

**3.** Trace the new pattern. You can make the same changes to the back bodice, if desired, and gather the entire waistline when sewing.

## ADDING FULLNESS GATHERED AT THE NECKLINE

**1.** Start with the pattern with the ungathered dart (page 67). Draw straight, evenly spaced lines radiating from the neckline as shown.

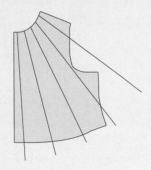

**2.** Starting at the neckline, slash the pattern, leaving a hinge at the bottom of each slash. Spread the pattern out evenly at the neckline. Shift the center front piece half the spread of the other pieces. Trace the new pattern.

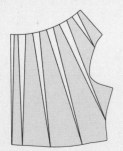 

**3.** When sewing you can gather at the neck only and leave the waist-dart space ungathered, or you can gather it also.

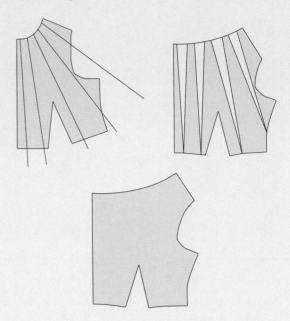

For a bodice with waist darts that is gathered at the neck, you can make the same changes to the pattern with the dart

# CREATING DART TUCKS

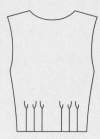

**1.** Start with the bodice pattern with the dart shifted to the armhole (page 62).

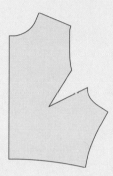

**2.** Draw 3 straight lines perpendicular to the waist below the dart. Connect each line to the tip of the dart.

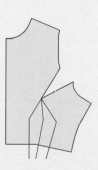

**3.** Slash the lines, leaving hinges. Spread the slashed pieces and close the armhole dart.

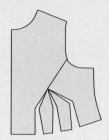

**4.** Trace the new pattern and mark the dart tuck lines (just the straight part of the line, not the part that connects to the dart tip). These are sewn along the straight lines the same way as a dart, only not as far.

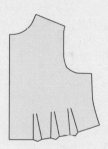

*secret garden party dress*

# THE STRAPLESS BODICE

A bold retro floral and a sexy strapless top meet a fun skirt. This dress
has a little bit of Southern charm and a whole lot of sass. All you need to
finish this look is a glass of iced tea. These instructions are for the
bodice with a lining and side zipper; alternatively, it can be made with a
facing and interfacing and a back zipper. My design pairs this bodice
with the gathered dirndl skirt (page 158).

## PATTERN PIECES

Center Front Strapless Bodice (sheet 1 back)
Side Front Strapless Bodice (sheet 1 back)
Center Back Strapless Bodice (sheet 1 back)
Side Back Strapless Bodice (sheet 1 back)

## YARDAGE

**FASHION FABRIC AND LINING FABRIC**
45" (114cm) fabric:
• Sizes 1 to 3: ½ yard (45.5cm)
• Sizes 4 to 12: ¾ yard (68.5cm)
60" (152.5cm) fabric:
• Sizes 1 to 12: ½ yard (45.5cm)

**TO FACE BODICE INSTEAD OF LINING, ADD**
¼ yard (23cm) of 45" (114cm) or 60" (152.5cm)
facing fabric
¾ yard (68.5cm) of 20" (51cm) interfacing

## SUPPLIES

2 yards (1.8m) of boning
invisible zipper

**notes**
• *Use a ⅝" (1.5cm) seam allowance for all sewing.*
• *If you make this with a back zipper, you will need to add a
⅝" (1.5cm) seam allowance to the center back pattern piece
and cut 2 center back pieces instead of 1 on the fold.*
• *The length of the zipper should be the length of the bodice
center-back seam or side seam (depending on where you
plan to insert it) plus 8" (20.5cm).*

## FABRIC TIP

The strapless bodice will work with a wide variety of fabrics
from thin, lightweight, and drapey to heavier and stiffer.
The lighter the fabric, the more the strapless bodice can
benefit from a lining (as opposed to a facing) in order to
give it structure.

## CUTTING LAYOUTS

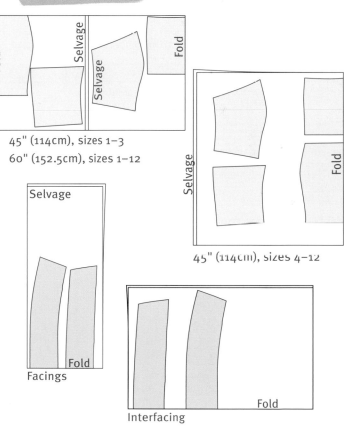

45" (114cm), sizes 1–3
60" (152.5cm), sizes 1–12

45" (114cm), sizes 4–12

Facings

Interfacing

**1.** Using the traced strapless bodice patterns on sheet 2, cut out the fashion fabric and lining according to the appropriate cutting layout for your fabric width and size.

**2.** Sew the side back pieces to the center back piece.

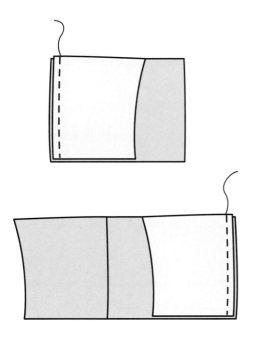

Repeat with the front pieces (if you'd like to add straps, see page 116) and the front and back lining pieces. Press the seams open.

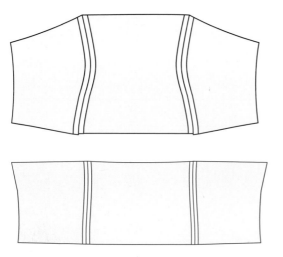

**3.** With right sides together, sew the fashion-fabric back bodice to the front bodice along one side seam. Press the seam open. Repeat with the lining.

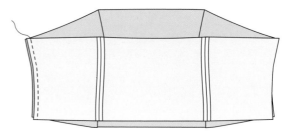

**4.** Add boning to the seams, if desired (page 32).

**5.** With right sides together, sew the lining to the fashion fabric along the top edge. Grade (page 35) and finish the seam allowances (page 36), if desired. Turn the bodice right side out and press.

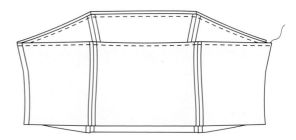

**6.** See page 32 for how to attach the skirt to the bodice.

# *beach bonfire dress*
# THE HALTER BODICE

Lightweight cotton was made for the dog days of summer. I love this blue-and-white Indian block print that gives this dress an easy-going, beachy vibe. When you want to let your hair down, nothing says "free spirit" like a halter style. These instructions are for the halter dress with a lining and a side zipper, but you can make it with a back zipper and/or a facing instead. It's paired with the pleated skirt (page 163) in the photograph.

## PATTERN PIECES

Front Halter Bodice (sheet 1 front)
Center Back Strapless Bodice (sheet 1 back)
Side Back Strapless Bodice (sheet 1 back)

## YARDAGE

**FASHION FABRIC AND LINING FABRIC**
45" (114cm) fabric:
• Sizes 1 to 12: 1 yard (0.9m)
60" (152.5cm) fabric
• Sizes 1 to 12: ¾ yard (68.5cm)

**TO FACE BODICE INSTEAD OF LINING, ADD**
¾ yard (68.5cm) of 45" (114cm) fabric or ½ yard (45.5cm) of 60" (152.5cm) facing fabric
¾ yard (68.5cm) of 20" (51cm) interfacing, for the front halter bodice
¾ yard (68.5cm) of 20" (51cm) interfacing, for the back halter bodice

## SUPPLIES

invisible zipper

## FABRIC TIP

The halter bodice will work with a wide variety of fabrics, from thin, lightweight, and drapey to heavier and stiffer; it just depends on the look you're after. See page 14 for more about fabrics.

## CUTTING LAYOUTS

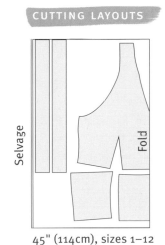

45" (114cm), sizes 1–12

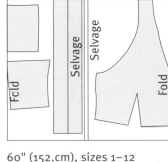

60" (152.cm), sizes 1–12

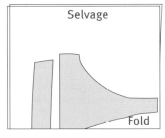

Facing, 45" (114cm)

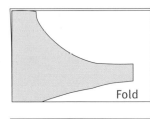

Interfacing

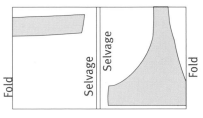

Facing, 60" (152.5cm)

• *Use a ⅝" (1.5cm) seam allowance.*
• *If you are using a back zipper instead of a side zipper, you will need to add a ⅝" (1.5cm) seam allowance to the center back pattern piece and cut 2 instead of 1 on the fold.*
• *The length of the zipper should be the length of the center-back bodice seam or side seam (depending on where you plan to insert it) plus 8" (20.5cm).*

**1.** Using the appropriate cutting layout for your fabric width and size, cut the fashion fabric and lining fabric using the traced halter pattern from sheet 1 front and both back strapless bodice patterns from sheet 1 back. Also cut two straps 2½" (6.5cm) wide by the desired length (they need to be long enough to tie around your neck) from both the fashion and lining fabric.

**2.** Begin by staystitching (page 22) the V-neck of the fashion-fabric halter. This will help to prevent it from stretching out and gaping. With right sides together, sew the fashion-fabric side back pieces to the center back piece to complete the halter back. Press the seams open.

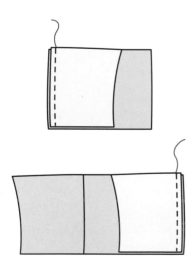

**3.** Sew the halter darts and press them toward the center.

**4.** With right sides together, sew the straps to the halter. Press the short ends of the straps to the wrong side by ⅝" (1.5cm). Press the seam open.

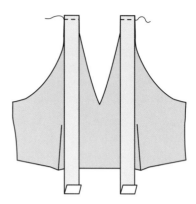

**5.** With right sides together, sew the halter back to the front along one side seam. Press the seam open.

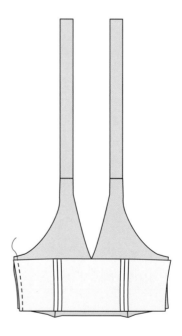

**6.** Repeat steps 2 through 5 with the lining fabric.

**7.** With right sides together, sew the lining to the fashion fabric along the top edge, including the neckline and the sides of the straps. Do not sew the side seams or the short ends of the straps.

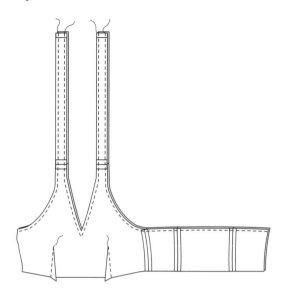

**8.** Grade the seams (see page 35) and clip the curves (see page 36). Clip the seam allowances at the point of the V-neck almost to the stitching line, but make sure not to cut through the stitching. Finish the seam allowances, if desired (see page 36).

**9.** Use a safety pin to turn both straps right side out, pulling the rest of the bodice with them. Press the bodice.

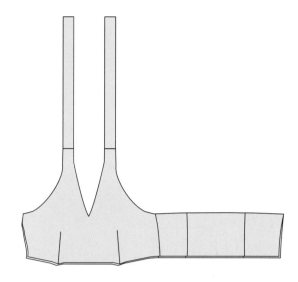

**10.** See page 32 for how to sew the skirt to the bodice.

# *vintage–style rockabilly dress*
# THE GATHERED DARTS AND YOKE VARIATION

Marilyn Monroe wore it in white in 1955. Reimagined in black, this style is a nod to the golden age of greasers and all-American good. You'll dream up new ways to use the same pattern with a few subtle alterations to the halter bodice, adding gathered darts and a yoke at the waist. It's paired here with the dirndl skirt (page 161).

**notes**
- *Use the same yardage amounts as for the Halter Bodice pattern (page 77).*
- *The cutting layout will also be the same as the halter bodice. The only difference is that the lower part of the front halter will be cut as a separate piece.*

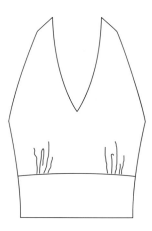

The finished halter bodice with gathered bust darts and a yoke

**1.** Raise the pointy tip of the dart straight up by ½" (13mm) and redraw the dart legs to the new bust point. Draw a line from the tip of the bust point to the armhole curve. Slash the line, shift the dart to the armhole curve, and close the waist dart. (See Pattern Design Spotlight: Dart Modifications, page 60.)

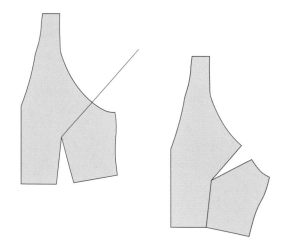

**2.** Measure from under your bust directly down to your waist. To make the yoke, draw a smooth curve across the midriff of the pattern at a point above the waistline that is less than the waist-to-underbust measurement you just took; remember to measure from the stitching line on the pattern. If the line is too high, the yoke will pass over the curve of your bust and the bodice won't fit right. Make sure that the line is perpendicular to the center front for at least ¼" (6mm).

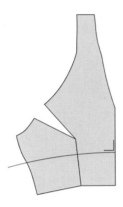

**3.** Cut the pattern along the yoke line. Tape the yoke pieces together. Draw several straight lines from the tip of the dart down to where the yoke seam line will be.

**4.** Slash the lines and close the dart at the armhole. Smooth out the angle of the yoke with a curve. Add a ⅝" (1.5cm) seam allowance to the top edge of the yoke.

**5.** Trace the new pattern shape and mark the gathering space with a dot on either side. Add a ⅝" (1.5cm) seam allowance to the bottom edge of the bodice.

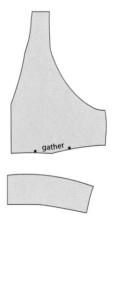
gather

**6.** Use the modified pattern to cut the fashion-fabric halter bodice and lining pieces. Gather the darts between the dots on both the fashion fabric and lining.

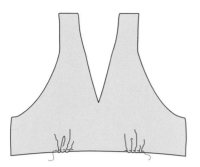

**7.** With right sides together, sew the fashion-fabric yoke to the bodice. Repeat with the lining fabric. Use the back bodice pattern for the back of the halter. Follow the basic sewing and assembly instructions for the basic halter bodice (page 77) to finish.

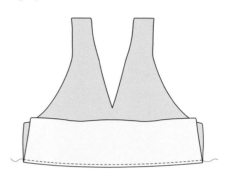

*studio 54 halter gown*

# THE GATHERED HALTER BODICE

This floor-sweeping number evokes Halston's timeless chic style, as epitomized by '70s icons Lauren Hutton, Liza Minnelli, and Bianca Jagger. Be ready to turn heads when you arrive at your formal event in this stunning style paired with a long bias skirt (page 150). These instructions are for a lined gathered halter bodice with a side zipper.

(page 150)

### PATTERN PIECES

Front Gathered Halter Bodice (sheet 1 back)
Center Back Strapless Bodice (sheet 1 back)
Side Back Strapless Bodice (sheet 1 back)

### YARDAGE

**FASHION FABRIC AND LINING FABRIC**
¾ yard (68.5cm) of 45" (114cm) or 60" (152.5cm) fabric, all sizes

### SUPPLIES

invisible zipper
safety pin

**notes**
- Use a ⅝" (1.5cm) seam allowance.
- The length of the zipper should be the length of the bodice's center-back seam or side seam (depending on where you plan to insert it) plus 8" (20.5cm).
- The cutting layout as shown will allow for a finished 1" (2.5cm) strap that is either 45" (114cm) or 60" (152.5cm) long, depending on your fabric.

### FABRIC TIP

The gathered halter bodice will work best with thin, lightweight, drapey fabric like silk, satin, or crepe. See page 14 for more about fabrics.

### CUTTING LAYOUT

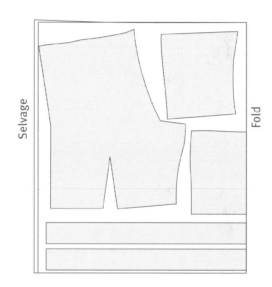

1. Trace and cut the pattern for the Front Gathered Halter Bodice from sheet 1 back and both back Strapless Bodice pattern pieces on sheet 1 back. Cut the fashion fabric and lining according to the cutting layout. Cut two 2¼" (5.8cm) wide strips from the fashion fabric only.

**2.** Sew the front bodice darts on the fashion fabric and lining pieces. Press the darts toward the center. On both the fashion fabric and lining pieces, make a mark with tailor's chalk or a dressmaker's pencil on the wrong side of the fabric where the center-front angle begins.

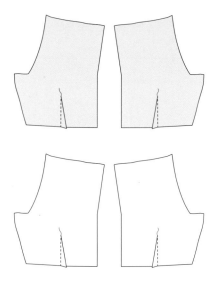

**3.** Sew one side back strapless piece to the center back piece. Sew the other side back strapless piece to the center back piece.

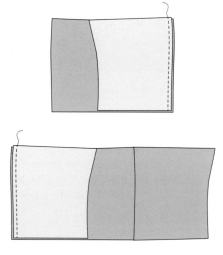

Repeat with the lining pieces. Press all the seams open.

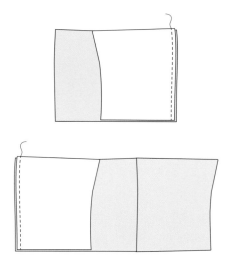

**4.** With right sides together, sew the back bodice piece to one front bodice piece along the side seam of both the fashion fabric and lining. Press the seams open.

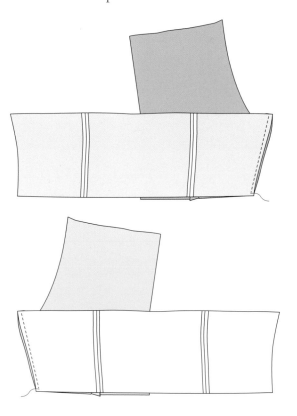

**5.** Open the bodice on both the fashion fabric and lining and, with right sides together, sew the bodice front pieces together along the top edge. Press the seam open.

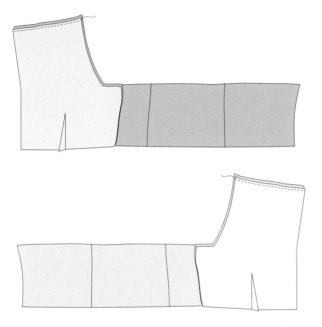

**6.** Open the bodice and lining and, with right sides together, sew along the center front between the marks you made in step 2, along the armhole curve, and across the top of the back bodice. Clip to but not through the stitching at the marks on the center front. Grade the seams (page 35) and clip the curves (page 36).

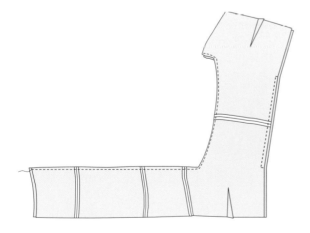

The gathered halter also works with a short, flirty circle skirt, as in the First Anniversary Dress. Find the instructions for this skirt on page 183.

**7.** Turn the bodice right side out. Flip the bodice over so that the right sides of the fashion fabric are facing each other and the right side of the lining is on the outside.

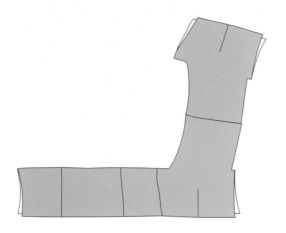

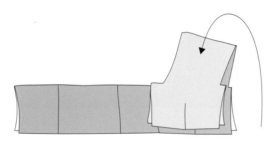

**8.** Fold the lining up on both sides so that the top portion of the bodice is sandwiched in between. With right sides together, sew the lining together along the unstitched portion of the center front, making sure not to catch any other part of the bodice in the stitches. Sew the fashion fabric right sides together along the center front. Press the seams open.

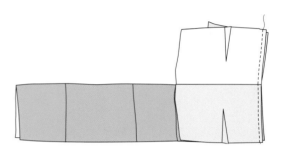

**9.** Make a neck tie by cutting 2 strips of fashion fabric 2¼" (5.5cm) wide by 45" (114cm)/60" (152.5cm) long. Press the short ends of each strip to the wrong side by ⅝" (1.5cm). With right sides together, sew along each long edge. Turn right side out with a safety pin and press. Topstitch (simply stitch on the right side of the fabric) the short ends closed. *Note:* You can tie the neck tie around your neck or sew it to the back bodice.

**10.** See page 32 for how to attach the skirt to the bodice.

*mix–and–match pattern design inspiration*

# BLUE SKIES DRESS

### (SHOWN WITH A ¾-CIRCLE SKIRT, SEE PAGE 185)

**1.** Start with the Mock-Wrap Bodice pattern (page 95). Draw a line from the neckline to the armhole for the upper yoke. Draw lines from the tip of the dart to the upper yoke line.

**2.** Slash the upper yoke line. Slash the lines to the dart tip but leave hinges at the tip. Close the waist dart and spread the slashed pieces for gathers (page 67). Measure from under your bust to your waist and add ⅝" (1.5cm) to this measurement. At a level above the waist that is 1" (2.5cm) less than this measurement, draw a line for the lower yoke across the bodice with the dart closed. Slash the lower yoke line.

**3.** To make the lower yoke pattern, trace the Halter Bodice pattern (pattern sheet 1) and shift the waist dart to the armhole (page 62). With the waist dart closed, draw a line across the bodice at the same level you did on the mock wrap.

**4.** Slash the line. Tape the yoke pieces together. Redraw the Mock-Wrap pattern for gathers (page 67) and add seam allowances to the edges that were slashed to complete the pattern.

Gather fabric more toward the front, with very little gathering at the sides.

*simple soirée dress*

# THE COWL NECK BODICE

When you want to look dressed up but not, you know, *too* dressed up, this simply elegant dress is at your service. A beautifully draped cowl neck is flattering on anyone, and it's easier to create than you might guess. These instructions are for the cowl bodice with facings and a side zipper. It's paired with the six-panel skirt (page 155) in the photograph.

## PATTERN PIECES

Cowl (sheet 3 front), traced and taped together to make a whole front pattern
Back Basic Bodice (sheet 1 front)

## YARDAGE

### FASHION FABRIC

45" (114cm) fabric:
• Cowl, sizes 1 to 12: 1 yard (0.9m)
• Back bodice, sizes 1 to 12: ¾ yard (68.5cm)
60" (152.5cm) fabric:
• Cowl and back bodice, sizes 1 to 8: 1 yard (0.9m)
• Cowl, sizes 9 to 12: 1 yard (0.9m)
• Back bodice, sizes 9 to 12: ¾ yard (68.5cm)

### FACING FABRIC

½ yard (45.5cm) of 45" (114cm) or 60" (152.5cm) fabric
¾ yard (68.5cm) of interfacing, 20" (51cm) wide

## SUPPLIES

invisible zipper

## FABRIC TIP

The cowl bodice is cut on the bias and will work best with a fabric that has a lot of drape and not much stiffness or body. See page 14 for more about fabrics.

## CUTTING LAYOUTS

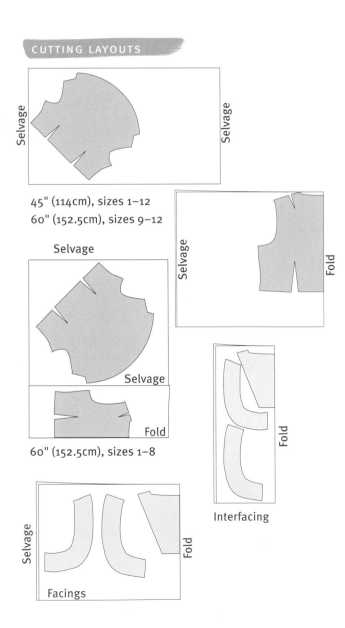

45" (114cm), sizes 1–12
60" (152.5cm), sizes 9–12

60" (152.5cm), sizes 1–8

Interfacing

Facings

**1.** Trace and cut the Cowl pattern from sheet 3 front. Trace again, flip it over, align center fronts, and tape together to make a whole Front Cowl Bodice pattern. Trace and cut the Back Basic Bodice pattern from sheet 1.

**2.** Make the extended facing pattern for the cowl neckline by tracing the top portion of the Cowl pattern as shown below. Cut out the tracing and tape the extended facing to the pattern as shown.

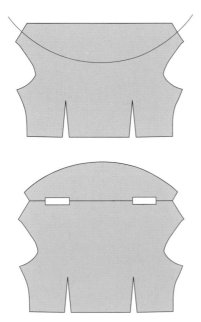

**3.** Make the back and front armhole facings (skip this step if you are adding a sleeve) by tracing the Cowl pattern and Back Basic Bodice pattern as shown to within ¹⁄₁₆"–⅛" (1mm–3mm) of the armhole curve. This will help the facing roll to the inside of the finished garment. (See page 25 for more about facings.) Make the back neckline facing by tracing the back neckline of the pattern as shown again, making sure to trace to within ¹⁄₁₆"–⅛" (1mm–3mm) of the neckline.

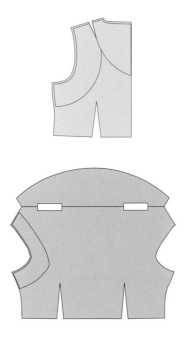

**4.** Cut the front cowl bodice from the fashion fabric using the extended pattern created in step 2. Cut the back bodice from the fashion fabric according to the appropriate cutting layout for your fabric width and size. Use the facing patterns to cut the facing fabric and the interfacing for the armholes and back neckline according to the cutting layout.

**5.** Interface the wrong sides of the armhole and back neck facing pieces according to the manufacturer's instructions. (See page 31 for more about interfacing.)

**6.** Sew the front darts of the cowl and press them toward the center. Sew the back bodice darts and press toward the center.

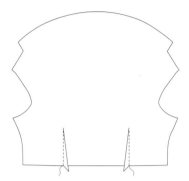

**7.** With right sides together, sew the back neck facing to the back bodice and press the seam open.

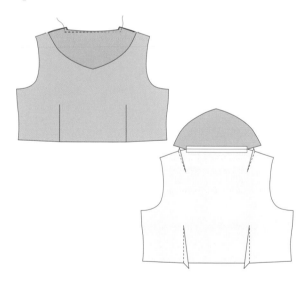

**8.** With right sides together, sew the front cowl bodice to the back bodice at the shoulder and along the facing as shown. Sew one side seam,

leaving the other side open for the zipper. Press the seam open.

**9.** With right sides together, sew the armhole facings together at the shoulder. Sew one pair at the side seam as well, making sure the facings with the open side seam are on the same side as the open side seam of the bodice. Press the seams open.

**10.** With right sides together, sew the armhole facings to the bodice. Grade the seams (page 35), clip the curves (page 36), understitch (page 36), and finish the seam allowances (page 36), if desired. Press neck and armhole facings to the inside.

**11.** See page 134 for how to attach sleeves, if desired. See page 32 for how to attach the skirt to the bodice.

*farmers' market frock*

# THE MOCK-WRAP BODICE

Sometimes you just need a go-to outfit when you have errands to run but still want to look nice. Enter the casual day dress—your weekend wardrobe's secret weapon. This mock wrap style is practical, cool, and helps you look effortlessly pulled together. These instructions are for the mock-wrap bodice with facings and a side zipper. It's shown in the photograph with the A-line skirt (page 178).

## PATTERN PIECES

Mock Wrap (sheet 2 back)
Back Basic Bodice (sheet 1 front)

## YARDAGE

FASHION FABRIC AND LINING FABRIC
45" (114cm) fabric:
- Sizes 1 to 6: 1 yard (0.9m)
- Sizes 7 to 12: 1¼ yard (1.1m)
60" (152.5cm) fabric:
- Size 1 to 12: ¾ yard (68.5cm)

TO FACE BODICE INSTEAD OF LINING, ADD
¾ yard (68.5cm) of 45" (114cm) or 60" (152.5cm) facing fabric
1 yard (0.9m) of 20" (51cm) interfacing

## SUPPLIES

invisible zipper

### notes
- *Skip the armhole facings if you will be adding a sleeve.*
- *Use a ⅝" (1.5cm) seam allowance for all sewing.*
- *If you make it with a back zipper instead of a side zipper, you will need to add a ⅝" (1.5cm) seam allowance to the center back of the Back Basic Bodice pattern and cut 2 instead of 1 on the fold.*
- *The length of the zipper should be the length of the bodice center-back seam or side seam (depending on where you plan to insert it) plus 8" (20.5cm).*

## FABRIC TIP

The mock-wrap bodice will work with many types of fabrics. See page 14 for more about fabrics.

## CUTTING LAYOUTS

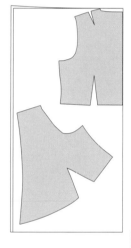

45" (114cm)

60" (152.5cm)

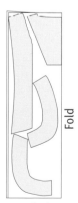

Interfacing

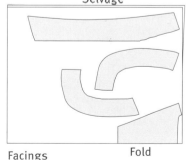
Facings

1. Trace and cut the pattern for the Mock-Wrap Bodice from sheet 2 back. Trace and cut the Back Basic Bodice pattern from sheet 1. Make the pattern for the facings by tracing the patterns as shown along the front and back armholes and necklines (see page 25 for more about facings). Make sure to trace to within ¹⁄₁₆"–¹⁄₈" (1mm–3mm) of the edge along the openings, which will ensure that your finished facing rolls to the inside of the garment instead of peeking out.

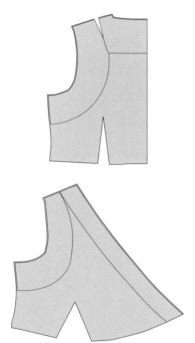

2. Cut the fashion fabric using the Mock-Wrap pattern and Back Basic Bodice pattern according to the appropriate cutting layout for your fabric width and size. Cut the facing fabric and interfacing according to the cutting layout.

3. Interface the wrong side of the facings according to the manufacturer's instructions. (See page 31 for more about interfacing.)

4. Sew the front darts and the back darts. Press all darts toward the center.

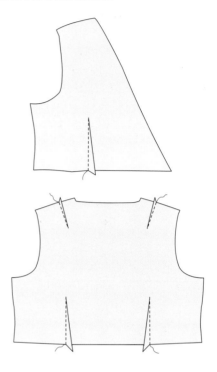

5. With right sides together, sew the front mock-wrap pieces to the back bodice at the shoulders and one side seam. Press the seams open.

**6.** With right sides together, sew the front neck facings to the back neck facing at the shoulder. With right sides together, sew the armhole facings together at the shoulder. Sew one set of armhole facings (the ones that will face the seam without the zipper) also at the side seam. Press all seams open.

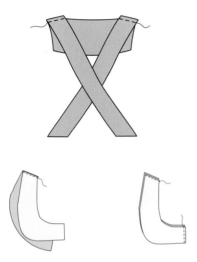

**7.** With right sides together, sew the facings to the neckline and armholes.

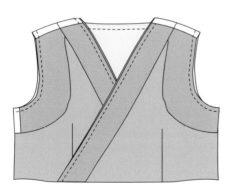

**8.** Grade the seam allowances (page 35), clip the curves (page 36), and understitch (page 36) the seam allowances to the facings. Finish the seam allowances (page 36), if desired. Press the facings to the inside of the bodice.

**9.** Arrange the bodice so that the points of the flaps extend 1 ⅝" (4cm) past each bust dart at the waist. Pin and sew the flaps together in this position.

**10.** See page 134 for how to attach sleeves, if desired. See page 32 for how to attach the skirt to the bodice.

*très brooklyn knit dress*
# THE PRINCESS BODICE

This "it girl" dress doesn't just look cool; it's also comfortable, easy to sew, and versatile enough to wear nearly anyplace. I love ponte because it wears like a knit but has enough body for designs with a bit more structure. These instructions are for the princess bodice with facings and a back zipper. It is shown with the half-circle skirt (page 184) in the photograph.

## PATTERN PIECES

Center Front Princess Bodice (sheet 2 front)
Side Front Princess Bodice (sheet 1 front)
Center Back Princess Bodice (sheet 2 front)
Side Back Princess Bodice (sheet 3 front)

## YARDAGE

FASHION FABRIC AND LINING FABRIC
45" (114cm) fabric:
• Sizes 1 to 12: 1 yard (0.9m)
60" (152.5cm) fabric:
• Sizes 1 to 8: ¾ yard (68.5cm)
• Sizes 9 to 12: 1 yard (0.9m)

TO FACE BODICE INSTEAD OF LINING, ADD
½ yard (45.5cm) of 45" (114cm) or 60" (152.5cm) facing fabric
1 yard (0.9m) of 20" (51cm) interfacing

## SUPPLIES

invisible zipper

notes
• *Skip the armhole facings if you will be adding a sleeve.*
• *Skip the armhole and neckline facings if you will be lining the bodice.*
• *Use a ⅝" (1.5cm) seam allowance for all sewing.*
• *The length of the zipper should be the length of the bodice center-back seam or side seam (depending on where you plan to insert it) plus 8" (20.5cm).*

## FABRIC TIP

The princess bodice will work with a wide variety of fabrics from thin, lightweight, and drapey to heavier and stiffer; it just depends on the look you're after. See page 14 for more about fabrics.

## CUTTING LAYOUTS

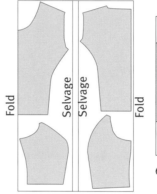

45" (114cm), sizes 1–12
60" (152.5cm), sizes 9–12

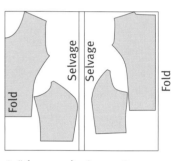

60" (152.5cm), sizes 1–8

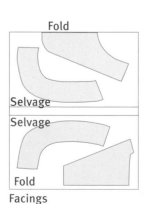

Facings

Interfacing

**1.** Trace and cut the Front and Back Princess Bodice pattern pieces from sheet 2 front.

**2.** Add a ⅝" (1.5cm) seam allowance for the zipper to the center back of the back bodice pattern if you will not be modifying the neckline to make it bigger with one of the neckline templates or the off-the-shoulder modification (page 103).

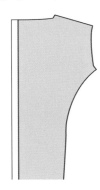

**3.** Cut the fashion fabric according to the appropriate cutting layout for your size and fabric width.

**4.** With right sides together, sew the side front pieces to the center front piece. Press the seams open. Repeat with the back pieces.

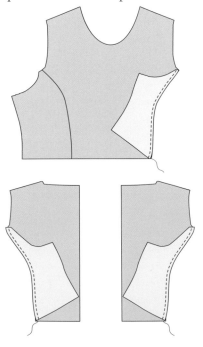

**5.** Trace the armhole and neckline of the sewn Front Princess Bodice to within ¹⁄₁₆"–⅛" (1mm–3mm) of the edge of the openings to make the pattern for the front facings (see page 25 for more about facings). Repeat with the sewn back bodice to make the facing patterns for the back armhole and neckline.

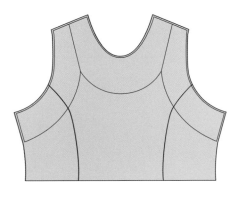

**6.** Cut the facing fabric and interfacing according to the appropriate cutting layout for your size and fabric width. Apply interfacing to the wrong side of the facings according to the manufacturer's instructions (see page 31 for more about interfacing).

**7.** Sew the front and back armhole facings with right sides together at the shoulder and side seams. Sew the front and back neckline facings together at the shoulder. Press all facing seams open.

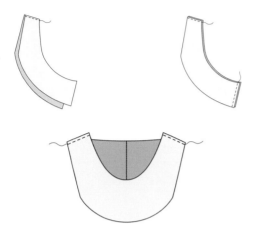

**8.** With right sides together, sew the front and back bodice together at the shoulder and side seams.

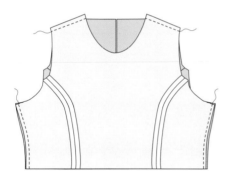

**9.** With right sides together, sew the armhole and neckline facings to the bodice. Grade the seams (page 35), clip the curves (page 36), understitch (page 36) the facing to the bodice seam allowance, and finish (page 36) the seam allowances, if desired. Press the facings to the inside of the bodice.

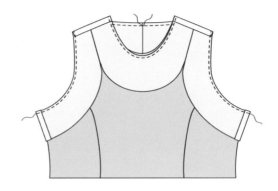

**10.** See page 134 for how to attach sleeves, if desired. See page 32 for how to attach the skirt to the bodice.

# *audrey high tea dress*
# THE OFF-THE-SHOULDER VARIATION

Inspired by the oh-so-flattering shoulder-skimming styles of the '50s,
this variation of the princess bodice is feminine and flirty, without a ruffle
in sight. Pair with a dreamy full-circle skirt (page 183), and you'll feel
like a classic movie star.

**notes**
- *If you're using 60" (152.5cm) fabric, you can use the same yardage amounts and cutting layouts as for the princess bodice (page 98).*
- *For 45" (114cm) fabric, you will need 1¼ yards (1.1m) of fabric for this design. Use a one-fold fabric layout. Cut 1 center front and 1 center back on the fold. Cut 2 side front pieces and 2 side back pieces.*

**1.** Trace the Center Front Princess Bodice pattern piece from sheet 2 front. With a ruler or straightedge, extend the line of the bust seam. Extend the line of the shoulder seam until it intersects with the extended bust seam line. Draw a smooth curve from the center front neck to the shoulder point. Now lower the angle of the extended shoulder line by ¼" (6mm); lowering the angle by ¼" (6mm) will allow for free movement of the arm. (If you would like the dropped shoulder to fit more closely to the arm, you can lower the angle more than ¼" [6mm]).

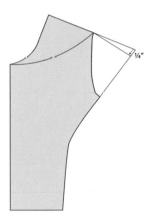

Cut out the new pattern.

**2.** Trace the Center Back Princess Bodice pattern piece from sheet 3. Lower the neckline along the center back by 2¾" (7cm). Draw a smooth curve from this point to the shoulder point. Make sure the first ¼" (6mm) of the curve is perpendicular to the center back. Extend the shoulder and back seam until they intersect as you did with the front pattern. Lower the shoulder angle by ¼" (6mm). Cut out the new pattern.

**3.** Place the new center back pattern on top of the new center front pattern and check the shoulder angle of the back pattern against the front and adjust it to match the front shoulder angle, if needed.

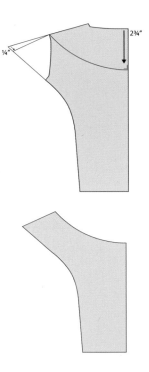

**4.** Follow the basic sewing instructions for the regular princess bodice (page 98).

# ·3·
# necklines and collars

A SIMPLE CHANGE TO A NECKLINE OF A DRESS CAN HAVE BIG style impact. Changing the shape of a neckline or adding a collar can make a basic dress design distinctive and unique. This chapter includes instructions and illustrations for how to use the scoop neck, V-neck, boatneck, and high V-neck neckline templates enclosed in the envelope at the back of the book in order to change the basic bodice or princess bodice necklines. It also includes instructions and illustrations for how to make patterns for and sew a Peter Pan, Johnny, mandarin, and band-type collar.

# *brocade highball dress*
# THE HIGH V-NECK

Cocktails, anyone? This dress screams '60s glamour, from the rich color to the classic silhouette with a straight skirt (page 169). Feel free to glam it up with an updo and dramatic earrings—this unusual neckline is like an eye-catching accessory unto itself. Use this same technique to modify the neckline of the basic or princess bodice with the V-neck or scoop-neck templates.

**1.** Trace the Front Basic Bodice pattern (sheet 1 front) or the Center Front Princess Bodice pattern (sheet 2 front). Cut the High V-Neck template from sheet 3 front. Place the template over the pattern, aligning the shoulder and center front.

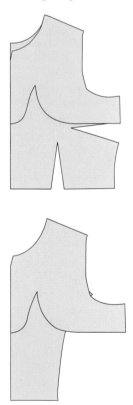

**2.** Trace the new neckline onto the pattern and cut out the new pattern.

*summer friday sheath*

# THE SCOOP NECK

A variation of the Day-to-Evening Sheath (page 49), this dress is a bit more playful, showing just a hint of collarbone. A crisp cotton with a bit of stretch makes it equally appropriate as a warm-weather look for the office. This dress shows how easy it is to create a new design by simply changing a single element. Here, I overlaid the Scoop Neck template onto the Front Basic Bodice pattern and kept everything else, including the straight skirt (page 169), the same as the original.

**1.** Trace the Front Basic Bodice pattern (sheet 1 front) or the Center Front Princess Bodice pattern (sheet 2 front). Cut the Scoop Neck template from sheet 3 front. Place the template over the pattern, aligning the shoulder and center front.

**2.** Trace the new neckline onto the pattern and cut out the new pattern.

*soda shop dress*

# THE DEEP V-NECK

This neckline is an incredibly flattering choice for many dress designs.
Overlaid here on the basic bodice, it is an easy way to change a pattern that
you already adore. The sweet retro fabric has a slightly old-fashioned yet
subtle print, so I chose to pair it here with a circle skirt (page 183).

**1.** Trace the Front Basic Bodice pattern or the Center Front Princess Bodice pattern. Cut the Deep V-Neck template from sheet 3 front. Place the template over the pattern, aligning the shoulder and center front.

**2.** Trace the new neckline onto the pattern and cut out the new pattern.

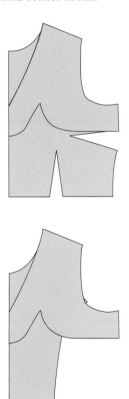

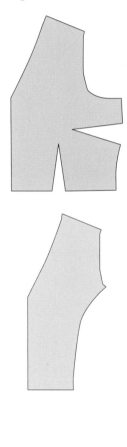

# *minimalist wedding gown*
# THE BOATNECK

When all eyes are on you, don't you want to be wearing something that just says "you"? Minimalists will love this sleek, simplified take on the traditional white dress with a long bias skirt (page 150), while the wide boatneck creates interest by beautifully framing the face and neck. To modify the neckline of the basic or princess bodices with the Boatneck template, you will need to modify both the front and back necklines of the pattern.

1. For the front neckline, trace the Front Basic Bodice pattern (sheet 1 front) or the Center Front Princess Bodice pattern (sheet 2 front). Cut the Boatneck template from sheet 3 front. Place the template over the pattern, aligning the shoulder and center front, and trace the new neckline.

2. For the back neckline of the basic bodice, trace the Back Basic Bodice pattern from sheet 1. Measure the shoulder seam length of the front Boatneck template and add ⅝" (1.5cm). Redraw the back bodice shoulder seam to this length from the shoulder point. Move the ⅝" (1.5cm) dart to the center of the new shoulder seam. Redraw the neckline with a smooth curve to the center back. Make sure the last ¼" (6mm) or so of new neckline is perpendicular to the center back.

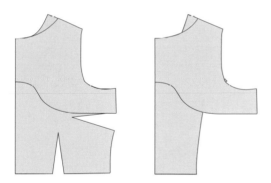

Cut out the new pattern.

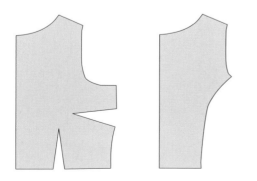

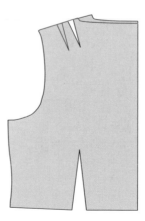

For the back neckline of the princess bodice, the procedure is the same as for the back basic bodice, but, as there is no dart, you won't be adding the ⅝" (1.5cm) for the dart to the shoulder-seam measurement.

# dotty for you dress
# THE SWEETHEART VARIATION

This va-va-voom silhouette is designed to get you attention. The casual cotton makes this dress more sophisticated and sweet than a more traditional evening-dress fabric might, and straps that tie in a bow at the neck provide extra support. This dress would even be cute for daytime wear under a jean jacket. Here, it's attached to the straight skirt (page 169).

**note**

• *You will use the same yardage amounts as for the strapless bodice (page 73). Add ¼ yard of fabric for the straps.*

1. Cut 4 strips from your fashion fabric that are 2¼" (5.5cm) wide by the desired length (or long enough to tie around your neck).

2. Attach a safety pin to the right side of one of the strips 1½" (3.8cm) from one of the short ends and parallel to the longer edges. With right sides together, sew another strip to the one with the safety pin along each long edge and the short edge that's closest to the safety pin, making sure not to sew over the pin. Grade the seam allowances (page 35) and clip the corners of the short sewn end. Turn the strap right side out by wiggling the safety pin toward the open short end. Repeat with the other two fabric strips, and press both.

**3.** On the Center Front Strapless Bodice pattern piece from sheet 1 back, draw a smooth curve from the center front, however low you want the dip of the sweetheart neckline to be, to the top of the bust seam and slash.

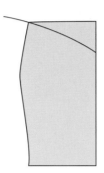

**4.** Because the sweetheart neckline is cut through the bias grain, you will need to staystitch (page 22) the neckline to prevent it from stretching out and gaping. Align the raw edges of the straps with the top raw edge of the right side of the sewn bodice front—anywhere you prefer—and stitch a little bit inside (closer to the raw edge) the ⅝" (1.5cm) seam allowance.

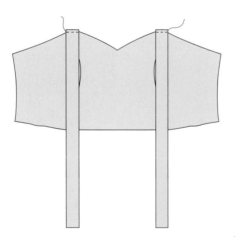

**5.** Follow steps 3–5 for the strapless bodice (page 73), keeping the straps in the downward position when you sew the lining to the bodice along the top edge. The straps will be sandwiched in between the fashion fabric and the lining.

# *collar drafting*

I t's amazing how much impact such a small detail as a collar can make to the design of a dress. Collars that stand up, like a band collar, or a shirt collar frame the neck in a flattering way. A flat, easy-to-make Peter Pan collar can be made in a contrasting color to interesting effect. A Johnny collar sewn to a V-neckline brings attention to the hollow of the neck. Some collars are sewn to the neckline in such a way that they cover the raw edge of the neckline, while some are sewn to the neckline in the same way a facing is attached. All collars help to set a dress apart, giving it a unique, detailed look.

Interfacing gives a collar a bit more stiffness and structure. (See page 31 for more about interfacing.) To use interfacing in your collar, apply it to the wrong side of the fashion fabric, according to the manufacturer's instructions, on the collar piece that shows the least. For example, to the mandarin or band collar, add interfacing to the piece that sits closest to the neck. For collars that lie flat, add it to the underside of the collar. You can also add it to both sides of the collar. This is especially useful when working with fabrics that are easily distorted, as the interfacing will ensure both sides of the collar are similarly stabilized. Remember to cut interfacing pieces along with your fashion fabric if you decide to use it.

Collars use a smaller seam allowance to cut down on bulk. Use a ⅜" seam allowance to sew the collar and to attach it to the bodice.

## THE BAND COLLAR

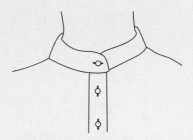

This style is just a band with no collar attached to it. It overlaps in the front for a button closure used with a front-opening bodice like a button-down. It covers the raw edge of the neckline when sewn to the bodice. You can use the existing Band collar pattern on sheet 2 back for this.

**1.** Cut 2 bands from your fashion fabric with the pattern's center back on the fold.

**2.** Trim the front and back bodice pattern necklines by ¼" (6mm) so they will match the ⅜" (1cm) seam allowance of the collar. Sew the collar pieces with right sides together using a ⅜" (1cm) seam allowance along the outside edge only; don't sew the neckline edge. Grade the seam allowances (page 35) and clip the curves (page 36). Turn right side out and press.

**3.** With right sides together, align one raw edge of the collar to the raw edge of the neckline and sew with a ⅜" (1cm) seam allowance. Press the unsewn raw edge of the collar to the inside by ⅜" (1cm). Flip the collar over the raw edge of the neckline. Sew close to the folded edge on the inside of the neckline. See the button-down bodice with collar on page 125 for an illustrated example of how to sew the band to cover the raw edge of the neckline. Make a buttonhole (page 34).

# THE JOHNNY COLLAR

A Johnny collar stands up a bit in the back but lies flat in front. It extends the desired amount down a V-neck and is sewn to the neckline in the same way as the Peter Pan (page 129) and mandarin collars (page 122). It will work with either a back- or side-zipper bodice. See page 112 for how to alter the basic bodice neckline using the Deep V-neck template on pattern sheet 3 front.

**1.** Draw the stitching line ⅝" (1.5cm) in from the edge of the front and back pattern neckline. Trim the ⅝" (1.5cm) seam allowance of the neckline by ¼" (6mm). Measure the back bodice's neck stitching line. Draw a rectangle 3" (7.5cm) wide and as long as the back neck measure.

**2.** Mark the stitching line of the front bodice shoulder ⅝" (1.5cm) in from the edge of the pattern. Measure down the front V-neck from the shoulder stitching line to the length that you want the finished collar to be. Extend the bottom line of the rectangle out this amount. Draw a perpendicular line up from this end 2½" (6.5cm). Connect this end back to the top of the original rectangle. Cut down from the top edge of the rectangle almost to the bottom, leaving a small hinge to pivot. Spread the cut, bending the rectangle, until the cut edges measure 1" (2.5cm) apart. Place paper behind

it and tape in place. Blend the edges of the cut with a slightly curved edge. Blend the corner at the bottom of the rectangle to a curve.

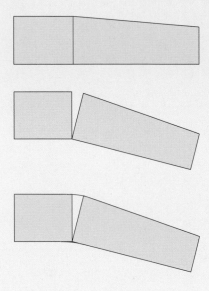

**3.** For a back-zip bodice, add ⅜" (1cm) seam allowances to all edges; cut 4 from the fashion fabric. For a side-zip bodice with a continuous collar, add a ⅜" (1cm) seam allowance to all edges except the center back. Cut 2 with the center back of the pattern on the fold.

**4.** With right sides together, sew the collar along all edges except the neckline edge. Grade (page 35) and clip (page 36) the seam allowances. Turn right side out and press. Align and sew both raw edges of the collar to the neckline.

**5.** Make a facing for the V-neckline (page 25). Remember to make the facing with a ⅜" (1cm) seam allowance, like the neckline. With right sides together, align and sew the raw edges of the facing to the raw edges of the collar and bodice neckline (the collar will be sandwiched in between). Grade the seams and clip the seam allowances at the point of the V, making sure not to cut through the stitching. Turn the facing to the inside and press. Refer to the Peter Pan collar (page 129) for an illustrated example of how to sew this type of collar to the neckline.

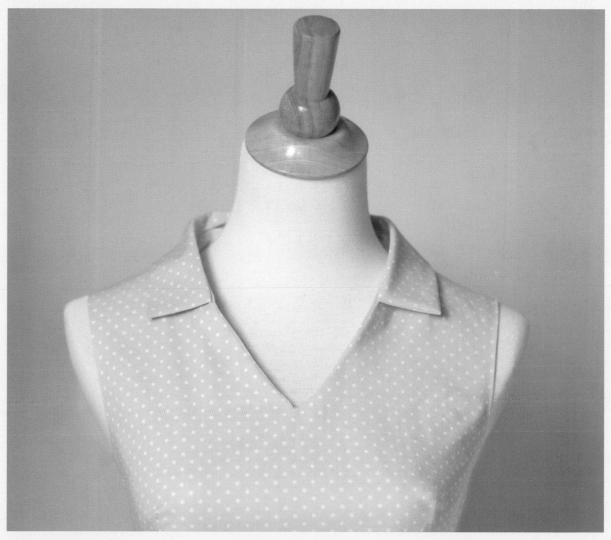

Johnny Collar closeup

*maggie rose dress*
# THE MANDARIN COLLAR

As a textile designer, I love the contrast between the clean lines of this dress and the romantic, painterly print. It is reminiscent of the '60s-era dresses worn by Maggie Cheung in *In the Mood for Love*. A mandarin collar is basically a band collar, but it does not overlap in the front. Instead of covering the raw edge of the neckline, the mandarin collar, like the Peter Pan collar, is sewn to the bodice with a facing.

**note**

• *This collar needs to be made with a back-zipper bodice. You won't be able to get your head through the neckline of a side-zipper bodice.*

**1.** To modify the Band Collar pattern on sheet 4 into a mandarin collar, measure back from the front edge 2" (5cm) and draw a line perpendicular to the edges. Draw a second line, ⅝" (1.5cm) back from the first line.

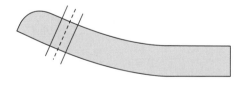

**2.** Fold the pattern so the 2 lines meet. Tape in place. Add a ⅜" (1cm) seam allowance to the center back of the pattern. Cut 4 from your fashion fabric.

**3.** Refer to the Peter Pan collar (page 129) for an illustrated example of how to sew this type of collar to the neckline. Trim the front and back bodice pattern necklines by ¼" (6cmm) so they will match the ⅜" (1cm) seam allowance of the collar. With right sides together, sew the collar pieces along the curved edge but not the neckline edge. Grade the seams (page 35) and clip the curves (page 36). Turn the collar right side out and press. Align and sew both raw edges of the collar to the neckline. Make a facing for the neckline (page 25).

**4.** Remember to make the facing with a ⅜" (1cm) seam allowance like the neckline. With right sides together, align and sew the raw edges of the facing to the raw edges of the collar and bodice neckline (the collar will be sandwiched in between). Grade the seams and clip the neckline curve, making sure not to cut through the stitching. Turn the facing to the inside and press.

The finished mandarin collar

*zigzag shirtdress*

# THE BUTTON-DOWN BODICE

The classic shirtwaist gets a modern update with a more relaxed silhouette and a fun, graphic print. Shown with a half-circle skirt (page 184) that is modified for a front-button closing (see step 14), it looks great with other skirts that have a hint of fullness. The button-down bodice is the perfect design to test your collar-drafting skills with any of the options in this chapter. These instructions are for the button-down bodice with collar and armhole facings.

## PATTERN PIECES

Front Basic Bodice (sheet 1 front)

Back Basic Bodice (sheet 1 front)

Button Extension (sheet 2 front)

Button Placement Template (sheet 2 back)

Collar and Band (sheet 2 back)

## YARDAGE

FASHION FABRIC

45" (114cm) fabric:

• Sizes 1 to 12: 1½ yards (1.4m)

60" (152.5cm) fabric:

• Sizes 1 to 9: ¾ yard (68.5cm)

• Sizes 10 to 12: 1½ yards (1.4m)

FACING FABRIC

½ yard (45.5cm) of 45" (114cm) or 60" (152.5cm) facing fabric

¾ yard (68.5cm) of 20" (51cm) interfacing

## SUPPLIES

Buttons

## FABRIC TIP

The button-down bodice will work well with a large variety of fabrics. See page 14 for more about fabrics.

## CUTTING LAYOUTS

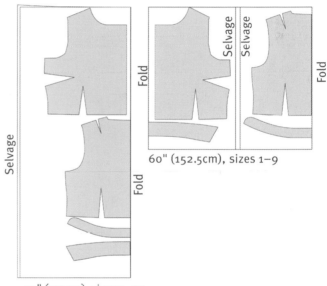

60" (152.5cm), sizes 1–9

45" (114cm), sizes 1–12
60" (152.5cm), sizes 10–12

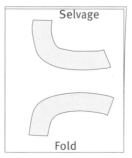

Facings

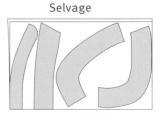

Interfacing

• *Skip the armhole facings if you will be adding sleeves.*
• *If you make the button-down bodice with only a front button-down opening—that is, without a back or side zipper extending through the skirt waist—then you will need to modify whichever skirt you pair it with to have the same kind of front-button opening (see step 14 below). If you don't, when you sew the skirt to the bodice, you won't be able to get the skirt over your hips. If you prefer not to modify the skirt in this way, then add a side or back zipper (remembering to add ⅝" [1.5cm] to the center back of the pattern) to the bodice in addition to the front-button opening.*
• *The seam allowances for the band, collar, and bodice neckline of this project are ⅜" (1cm). All the other seam allowances are ⅝" (1.5cm).*

1.  Trace and cut the Front and Back Basic Bodice patterns from sheet 1. Trace and cut the Button Extension from sheet 2 front. Trace and cut the Collar and Band patterns from sheet 2 back. Trace and cut the Button Placement Template from sheet 2 back.

2.  Tape the button extension to the center front of the bodice pattern. Trim the neckline of the Front and Back Basic Bodice pattern necklines by ¼" (6mm).

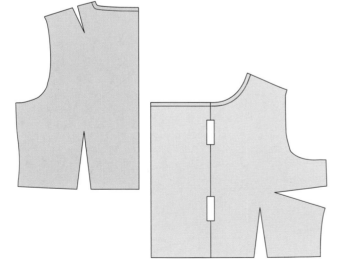

3.  Make the facing pattern for the front and back armholes by tracing the pattern (page 25).

4.  Cut the fashion fabric, facing fabric, and interfacing according to the appropriate cutting layout for your fabric width and size.

5.  With right sides together, sew the collar along the side and top edges using a ⅜" (1cm) seam allowance. Clip the corners without cutting through the stitches. Turn collar right side out and press.

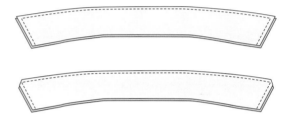

6.  Place the two band pieces right sides together. Place the collar in between and, with raw edges aligned, pin and sew the band to the collar using a ⅜" (1cm) seam allowance. Clip the curves (page 36), turn the band right side out, and press.

**7.** Sew the darts on the front bodice pieces. Press the bust darts down and the waist darts toward the center. Sew the back bodice darts and press toward the center.

**8.** Press the button extension on both front bodice pieces to the wrong side by the amount marked on the pattern; repeat and stitch close to the folded edge. With right sides together, sew the shoulder and side seams. Press the seam open.

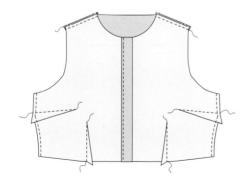

**9.** Turn the bodice right side out and place the Button Placement template on one of the button extensions, lining it up with the folded edge. Mark the buttons for your chosen size according to the template with tailor's chalk or a dressmaker's pencil. Repeat on the other button extension.

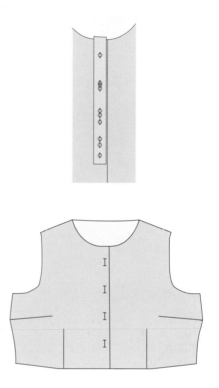

**10.** Apply the interfacing to the wrong side of the facing fabric according to the manufacturer's instructions (see page 31 for more info). With right sides together, sew the front and back armhole facings at the shoulder and side seams. Press the seams open.

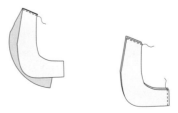

**11.** Sew the armhole facings to the bodice with right sides together.

**12.** With right sides together, pin and sew one side of the collar band to the neckline using a ⅜" (1cm) seam allowance.

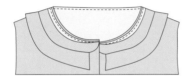

Press the remaining raw edge of the band to the inside by ⅜" (1cm). Flip the band over the raw edge of the neckline. Pin and stitch close to the folded edge on the inside of the neckline.

**13.** Grade the seams (page 35), clip the curves, and finish the seam allowances (page 36), if desired. Turn the armhole facing to the inside of the bodice and press.

**14.** To make the dress as shown, make the one-seam half-circle skirt (page 184) but don't add the seam allowances. Instead, extend the seam allowances the same amount as the button extension used for the bodice. Fold the seam allowances to the wrong side twice by the same amount you did on the bodice button extension. Sew close to the folded edge. Space the buttons the same amount apart as on the bodice pattern.

*zooey fit-and-flare dress*
# THE PETER PAN COLLAR

This adorable collar style isn't just reserved for schoolgirls. The Peter Pan collar has seen a revival on the necks of sophisticated women, and it's an easy way to switch up the look of a dress combination that you love and wear frequently. Contrast the sweetness of the Peter Pan with a more sedate dress, like this black-and-white striped style that pairs the basic bodice (page 49) with the box-pleat variation of the pleated skirt (page 166).

**notes**

• *A Peter Pan collar lies flat against the bodice. It can be made with either a front- (like a button-down) or back-opening bodice. If you make it for a side-zipper bodice, you won't be able to get your head through the neckline so don't do that.*

• *This collar is made with a ⅛" (1cm) seam allowance. Trim the bodice pattern neckline by ¼" (6mm) so it will match the ⅛" (1cm) seam allowance of the collar. When a facing is called for, remember to also make the facing's seam allowance ⅛" (1cm).*

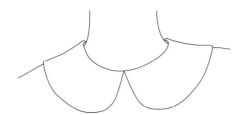

The finished Peter Pan collar

**1.** To make the pattern, first trim the front and back bodice pattern neckline by ¼" (6mm) so that the finished seam allowance will be ⅜" (1cm). Mark the shoulder stitching lines of your bodice pattern ⅝" (1.5cm) in from the edge and tape the front bodice to the back bodice, lining up the marked neck stitching line (the seam allowances will be overlapped). At about a 45-degree angle to the center front of the bodice, mark 3" (7.5cm). At a 45-degree angle to the center back, mark out 2" (5cm). Along the shoulder line, mark out 2½" (6.5cm). Starting at the center-front neckline, curve out to the 3" (7.5cm) mark, the shoulder mark, and the 2" (5cm) mark on the back, ending at the center-back neckline.

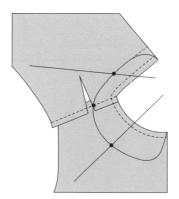

**2.** Add a ⅜" (1cm) seam allowance to the outer edges only, since the seam allowance on the neck edge is already there. This is the classic Peter Pan collar in two halves. If you wish to have one continuous collar (as you might with a front-opening button-down bodice for instance), simply continue perpendicular from the 2" (5cm) mark to the center back (as shown by the dotted line in the diagram below) and do not add the seam allowance to the center back of the pattern piece. If making a continuous collar do not add the seam allowance to the center back of the pattern.

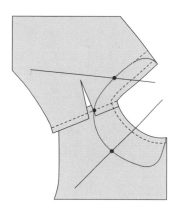

**3.** For a collar in halves, cut 4 from your fashion fabric. For a continuous collar on a front-opening bodice, cut 2 on the fold from your fashion fabric.

**4.** Sew the collar pieces, with right sides together, along the outside edge (don't sew the neckline edge) using a ⅜" (1cm) seam allowance. Grade the seam allowances (page 35) and clip the curves (page 36). Turn right side out and press. Align and sew both raw edges of the collar to the neckline.

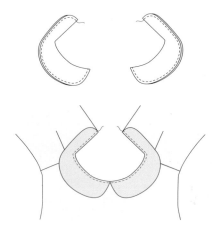

**5.** Make a facing for the neckline (page 25). Remember to make the facing with a ⅜" (1cm) seam allowance like the neckline. With right sides together, align and sew the raw edges of the facing to the raw edges of the collar and bodice neckline (the collar will be sandwiched in between).

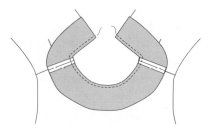

**6.** Grade the seams and clip the neckline curve, making sure not to cut through the stitching. Turn the facing to the inside and press.

# ·4·
# sleeves

WHILE IT IS TRUE THAT SEWING A SET-IN SLEEVE CAN BE A BIT of a finicky undertaking, it really isn't that difficult. As with all things in sewing, practice will give you the confidence to know that this is yet another thing that you can definitely do. If you haven't sewn a sleeve before, I recommend practicing a bit with a muslin (page 24) before taking on the real thing. Patterns for the cap sleeve, short sleeve, three-quarter sleeve, and long sleeve can be found in the envelope at the back of the book, and all four of them use the same basic technique. Even more design techniques will allow you to change the basic sleeve patterns to create puffed sleeves, bell sleeves, and split sleeves—all included in this chapter's Pattern Design Spotlight.

And here's a secret: You can avoid sewing a set-in sleeve altogether by changing the bodice pattern to include an all-in-one sleeve. Instructions for an all-in-one cap sleeve and an all-in-one kimono sleeve are included in this chapter as well.

*city chic lbd*

# THE CAP SLEEVE

Oh, the little black dress. If there is one dress you need in your closet, this is it. The cap sleeve makes it versatile for work and play, along with the basic bodice (page 49) modified with the boatneck (page 115) and a straight skirt (page 169).

(page 49) (page 115) (page 169)

## YARDAGE

**LONG SLEEVE**
• ¾ yard (68.5cm) of 45" (114cm) or 60" (152.5cm) fabric, 1 fold layout

**THREE-QUARTER SLEEVE**
• ¾ yard (68.5cm) of 45" (114cm) or 60" (152.5cm) fabric, 1 fold layout

**SHORT SLEEVE**
• ½ yard (45.5cm) of 45" (114cm) or 60" (152.5cm) fabric, 1 fold layout

**CAP SLEEVE**
• Sizes 1 to 6: ¼ yard (23cm) of 45" (114cm) or 60" (152.5cm) fabric, 1 fold layout
• Sizes 7 to 12: ½ yard (45.5cm) of 45" (114cm) or 60" (152.5cm) fabric, 1 fold layout

**note**
• *Use a ⅝" (1.5cm) seam allowance for all sewing.*

*Sewing instructions for all sleeves*

**1.** Trace and cut your chosen long, three-quarter, short, or cap sleeve from pattern sheet 2 back.

**2.** With the fabric folded, lay the pattern on top and cut 2 sleeves from the fashion fabric. Transfer notches on the top curve of the shoulder (sleeve cap) using tailor's chalk or a dressmaker's pencil. There is one notch at the front shoulder, one at the center shoulder, and two notches at the back shoulder. These same notches are marked on the bodice pattern (one notch at the front of the armhole and two at the back armhole), allowing you to line up these notches when pinning and sewing the sleeve to the bodice. Use the bodice pattern to mark the notches on your sewn bodice.

**3.** Sew a line of basting stitches by hand or machine between the front and back notches. Do not backstitch.

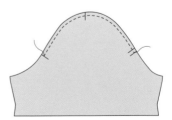

Gather very slightly between the notches. This small amount of gathering provides a little more space at the shoulder and allows for more comfortable movement of the arm. It also gives the sleeve a tiny bit of height at the shoulder, which is aesthetically pleasing.

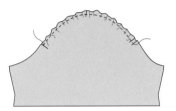

**4.** With right sides together, fold the sleeve and sew the underarm seam. Press the seam open.

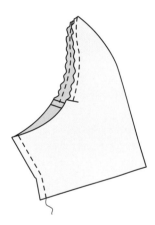

**5.** With your bodice inside out, pin the sleeve to the inside of the armhole with right sides together. Make sure to align the front and back sleeve notch markings with the front and back bodice armhole notch markings, the sleeve shoulder notch with the shoulder seam of the bodice, and the underarm seam of the sleeve with the side seam of the bodice. Take your time with this and make sure that the slight gathering at the top of the sleeve is evenly distributed between the notches. Sew the sleeve to the bodice. Do this slowly and in short bursts so that you can keep the seam flat under your needle as you sew around the armhole. Before removing the basting stitches, take a look at the sleeve and make sure the slight gathers at the shoulder look evenly distributed with no major puckers.

**6.** Finish the hem of the sleeve by serging or zigzag-stitching the raw edge. Press to the inside by ⅝" (1.5cm) and stitch close to the finished edge. Clip the curves (page 36) and finish the seam allowances (page 36), if desired.

*mix-and-match pattern design inspiration*

# MODERN APRON DRESS

(SHOWN WITH A ¾-CIRCLE SKIRT, SEE PAGE 185)

When you've mastered the pattern modifications featured in the Pattern Design Spotlights throughout the book, try these combinations of the techniques.

**1.** Use the Basic Bodice pattern (page 49) and shift the bust dart to the waist (page 61).

**2.** Add the cap sleeve to the pattern (page 145).

**3.** Draw the lines as shown. Cut through the lines and discard the lower neckline piece.

**4.** Add ⅝" (1.5cm) seam allowances to all the lines that were cut, including the dart, as the dart has become a seam. Trace the new pattern pieces.

# *mix-and-match pattern design inspiration*
# MINT DREAMS DRESS
## (SHOWN WITH A ¾-CIRCLE SKIRT, SEE PAGE 185)

After mastering the pattern modifications discussed throughout the book in the Pattern Design Spotlights, give these technique combinations a try.

**1.** Use the Basic Bodice pattern (page 49) and shift the bust dart to the waist (page 61).

**2.** Add the cap sleeve to the pattern (page 145). Draw lines as shown.

**3.** Slash the sleeve, through the top of the bodice to the neckline as shown, to create a yoke. Discard the bottom part of the sleeve. Slash the lines that extend from the tip of the dart but leave small hinges at the tip. Close the waist dart, spread the pieces for gathers (page 67), and trace the new shape. Add ⅝" (1.5cm) seam allowances to the bottom of the sleeve, the bottom of the yoke, and the edge that will be gathered to complete the pattern. Gather fabric more toward the front, with very little gathering at the sides.

## *autumn in new york dress*
# THE SHORT SLEEVE

Depending on where you live, early fall days can be the most difficult to dress for. Between chilly mornings and sunny afternoons, who knows what the weather may bring? Short sleeves help solve this dilemma: You can choose a tweedy, heavier fabric such as this plaid but feel free to go for a walk on your lunch break. Use the instructions found with the cap sleeve (page 134) on the basic bodice (page 49), and complete the look by drafting a half-circle skirt (page 184).

# *first day at the office dress*
# THE THREE-QUARTER SLEEVE

The key to acing a job interview is a killer résumé, a firm handshake, and, of course, a perfectly polished outfit. Be prepared to make a good impression with this structured dress that really shows the major impact that changing a few details can make in a dress design. Start with the basic bodice (page 49) and follow the instructions to create a new neckline with the deep V-neck template (page 112). Create your three-quarter-length sleeve following the instructions for the cap sleeve (page 134) and attach a straight skirt (page 169).

*skater ponte dress*

# THE LONG SLEEVE

When the thermometer drops, you'll want to cover up without sacrificing style. Enter this long-sleeved style in a heavier knit fabric, paired with a half-circle skirt (page 184). Ponte is available in a range of hues. Try a vibrant jewel tone and watch it chase away the winter blues. Use the long-sleeve pattern and the sewing instructions with the City Chic LBD (page 134) to create the long sleeves and set them into the princess bodice (page 98).

# sleeve modifications

## PUFFED SLEEVE

**1.** Trace and cut out the sleeve pattern of your choice. Transfer the front, back, and shoulder sleeve notches to the new pattern.

**2.** Cut off the ⅝" (1.5cm) hem allowance.

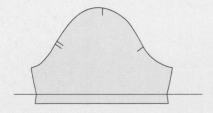

**3.** Draw parallel straight lines from the front, back, and shoulder notches. And 2 more lines between the front and shoulder notches and the shoulder and back notches. Slash the pattern along the lines.

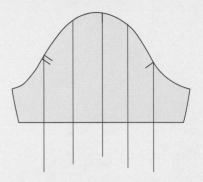

**4.** Spread the pattern evenly to the desired puffiness. Begin with a 1" (2.5cm) spread between each piece. Redraw the shoulder curve (sleeve cap) so that it extends upward from the original center shoulder notch by 1" (2.5cm). Extend the hem downward by 1" (2.5cm).

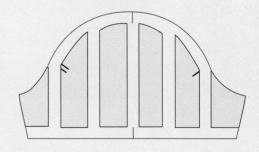

**5.** Add a ⅝" (1.5cm) seam allowance to the hem.

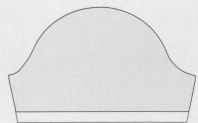

# PUFFED SLEEVE BAND

**1.** To add a ½" (13mm) band for a puffy sleeve, cut a strip of fabric that is the same measurement as the hem of the original sleeve pattern (after the seam allowance was cut off) by 1⅝" (4cm).

**2.** Hand- or machine-baste between the front and back shoulder notches and at the hem. Gather the shoulder curve (sleeve cap) between the notches. Gather the hem to the same size as the band.

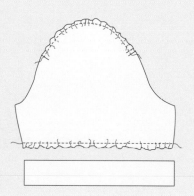

**3.** With right sides together, sew the band to the bottom of the sleeve.

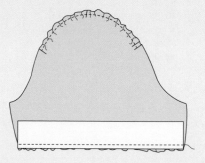

**4.** With right sides together, fold the sleeve and sew the underarm seam. Press the seam open.

**5.** Press the band to the wrong side by ½" (13mm). Repeat and sew close to the folded edge.

## PUFFED SHOULDERS ONLY

**1.** To modify any of the sleeve patterns for a sleeve that is puffy at the shoulder but not at the hem, follow steps 1–3 for the Puffed Sleeve (page 142) but slash from the shoulder and do not cut all the way through the hem. Instead leave small hinges.

**2.** Spread the sleeve evenly at the shoulder. Redraw the shoulder curve (sleeve cap) so that it extends upward from the original center shoulder notch by 1" (2.5cm).

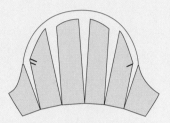

**3.** Add a ⅝" (1.5cm) seam allowance to the hem. Because of the inward curve of the hemline, this sleeve will need to be faced rather than hemmed. See page 25 for more about facings.

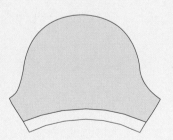

## BELL SLEEVE

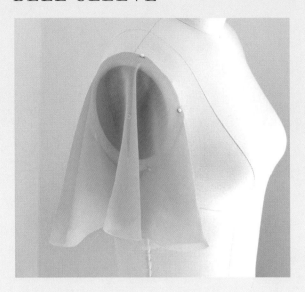

**1.** To modify any of the sleeve patterns for a bell-shaped sleeve, repeat steps 1–3 for the Puffed Sleeve (page 142) but slash from the hem and do not slash all the way through the shoulder curve. Instead leave small hinges.

**2.** Spread the sleeve evenly at the hem and add 1" (2.5cm) of length.

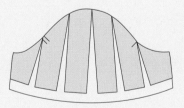

**3.** Add a ⅝" (1.5cm) seam allowance to the hem.

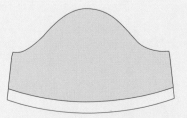

## SPLIT BELL SLEEVE

**1.** Follow steps 1–3 for the Bell Sleeve (previous page).

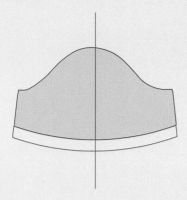

**2.** Slash the pattern at the center shoulder notch.

**3.** Add a ⅝" (1.5cm) seam allowance to the center front pieces.

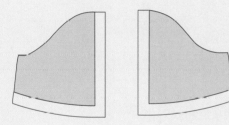

## ALL-IN-ONE CAP SLEEVE

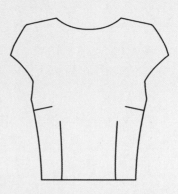

The basic bodice and sleeve patterns can be joined to make a pattern that is cut all in one with the bodice. The advantage is that you don't have to cut or sew a set-in sleeve, making the process a little quicker. The all-in-one cap sleeve is sewn front to back using an overarm seam, extending only part of the way down the armhole.

**1.** To make the pattern for the all-in-one cap sleeve, trace the Front and Back Basic Bodice patterns from sheet 1. Cut off the ⅝" (1.5cm) seam allowance on both the front and back bodice armhole curves. Trace one of the sleeve patterns from sheet 2 back; you only need the sleeve-cap portion of the sleeve, so any of the sleeve patterns will do.

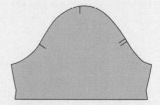

**2.** Draw a straight line down from the shoulder point notch. Draw a line from the front sleeve notch (one notch) to the back sleeve notches (two notches).

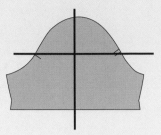

**3.** Cut out the front and back sleeve caps. Mark and cut off the ⅝" (1.5cm) seam allowances from the sleeve cap curves. Mark them front and back and make a mark at the shoulder point on each to indicate where the shoulder is.

**4.** On both the front and back bodice, align the appropriate sleeve cap so that the curve of the sleeve cap is touching the armhole curve and the shoulder point of the sleeve cap is ½" (13mm) away from the shoulder point of the bodice. The shoulder points of the bodice and sleeve cap should be parallel to each other.

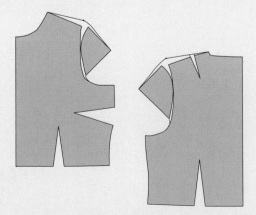

**5.** Raise the shoulder point of the bodice by ¼" (6mm). Draw a curve to the sleeve hem from this point. Connect the raised shoulder point to the neckline. On the back bodice, extend the shoulder dart to the new shoulder line. Draw a slight curve at the bottom of the sleeve to blend it into the armhole, which will also be easier to sew than an angle. Add ⅝" (1.5cm) hem allowance to the sleeve and the remainder of the armhole to finish the pattern. Sew the darts and then with right sides together, sew the shoulder seams and side seams.

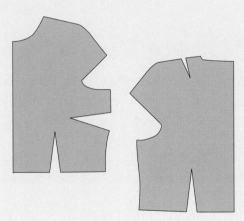

# KIMONO SLEEVE

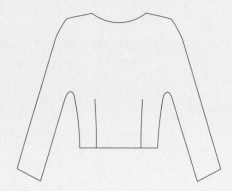

The kimono sleeve was quite popular in the '40s and '50s. Just look at how many of the patterns from that time show a sleeve that is not sewn to the bodice but is all in one with the bodice and sewn front to back with an overarm seam. It is certainly a stylish solution to avoid sewing a set-in sleeve!

1.  To make the pattern for the kimono sleeve, start by tracing the Front and Back Basic Bodice patterns from sheet 1. Shift the bust dart to the waist (page 61). Trace the desired sleeve pattern. Any of them will work; it just depends on your preferred length. Cut off the ⅝" (1.5cm) hem allowance of the sleeve.

2.  Align the front and back bodice so that they are touching at the neckline and the front shoulder is spread ½" (13mm) from the back shoulder seam. Don't worry about the shoulder dart. This design has some wearing ease under the arm that will allow the arm to move comfortably. Align the sleeve pattern at the armhole so that the underarm curve of the sleeve is touching the side seam of the front and back bodice equally. Tape in place. Draw a line from the neckline where the front and back are touching to the middle of the sleeve hem. Make a mark 1½" (3.8cm) diagonally from the

underarm. Extend the width of the sleeve hem by ⅝" (1.5cm) on each side. Draw a smooth curve from the side-seam waist to the underarm mark to the extended sleeve hem on both the front and back.

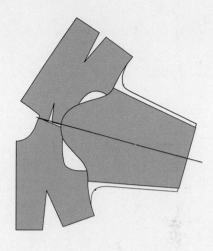

3.  Add the sleeve hem allowance by tracing the hem allowance of the original sleeve pattern, extending the width by ⅝" (1.5cm) on each side to match the new width of the sleeve.

4.  Trace the new pattern and cut apart along the line from the neckline to the sleeve hem. When sewing, sew the front to the back with right sides together along the side seams, the underarm seam, and the overarm seam.

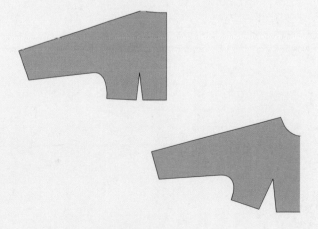

# ·5·
# skirts

THIS CHAPTER PROVIDES ILLUSTRATIONS AND INSTRUCTIONS FOR the bias-cut gown skirt, the straight skirt, and the flared six-panel skirt. The patterns for these can be found in the envelope at the back of the book. Instructions are also given for how to create the pattern for the full-, half-, three-quarter-, and quarter-circle skirts, as well as a simple gathered or pleated skirt. See page 32 for how to sew the skirt to the bodice, and page 33 for how to insert the zipper. Pattern alterations to achieve a better fit for your skirt are described on page 199.

Any of the skirts in this chapter can be made as a stand-alone skirt by adding a waistband; see page 187 for directions. Illustrations and instructions for easy pattern design techniques are also included in the Pattern Design Spotlight section of this chapter (page 172). There you will find simple techniques to modify the basic straight skirt pattern to make an A-line or full hem skirt, a wrap skirt, and a combination gathered/A-line skirt.

# *night at the opera gown*
# THE BIAS SKIRT

Steal the show when you make an entrance in this dramatic gown with classic, Old Hollywood glamour. These instructions are for the bias skirt with a side zipper, but you can make it with a back zipper instead without modifying the pattern. It's shown in the picture with the lined strapless bodice (page 73). If you're new to sewing skirts on the bias, make sure to review my general notes on bias garments (page 152).

(page 73)
(page 152)

## PATTERN PIECES

Bias Skirt Front Pieces 1 and 2 taped together (sheet 3 back)
Bias Skirt Back Pieces 1, 2, and 3 taped together (sheet 3 back)

## YARDAGE

**FASHION FABRIC AND LINING FABRIC**
3½ yards (3.2m) of 60" (152.5cm) fabric, all sizes

## SUPPLIES

invisible zipper

### notes

• *Bias garments are cut from a whole as opposed to a half pattern. They are not cut on a fold. The front skirt pattern on the pattern sheet is cut in half only to save space. You will need to tape together and trace front pattern pieces 1 and 2, and then trace them again to make a whole front pattern. Or, trace around the taped together half pattern with tailor's chalk or a dressmaker's pencil directly onto the fabric, then lift and flip the pattern to trace the remaining side of the skirt. You will need to trace, cut out, and tape together the 3 pieces that make up the back bias skirt pattern on the pattern sheet.*
• *The zipper length should be 8" (20.5cm) plus either the length of the bodice center back for a back zipper or the length of the bodice side seam for a side zipper.*

## FABRIC TIP

This skirt will work well with fluid, drapey, light- to medium-weight fabrics. Crepe is often great to use with bias-cut garments as it has these qualities but is also very stable due to its tight weave.

## CUTTING LAYOUT

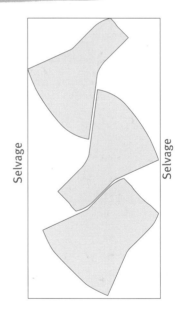

Selvage

Selvage

# notes on the bias

This skirt is really easy and simple in terms of construction, but its bias cut can still be tricky. Cutting it on the bias allows the fabric to stretch around the body, which is great for fitting over curves without darts. But bias-cut garments also stretch downward, which can cause all manner of problems from twisty seams to an altered fit. Here are a few possible ways to avoid those problems.

## MAKE A MUSLIN!

It's really, really important to make a muslin first (page 24) in an inexpensive fabric but one that is as similar as possible to the fabric you plan to use. You really need to make the muslin to see what problems might occur.

## HANG THE FABRIC.

You should always hang fabric you plan to use on the bias (it won't do any good to hang it on the straight grain) for about a week before cutting it. This will ensure that it has done a lot of its downward stretching before you cut it.

## HANG THE SEWN SKIRT BEFORE HEMMING.

After you sew the skirt, let it hang for a few days before hemming to ensure an even hem.

## INCREASE THE SEAM ALLOWANCES.

Even if you make a successful muslin first, without using the exact same fabric as you did for the muslin, the final bias skirt may have problems. Increasing the seam allowances from the built-in ⅝" (1.5cm) seam allowance to 2" (5cm) or even 3" (7.5cm) allows reshaping of the side seams if necessary. See page 199 for more on alterations.

## PICK THE RIGHT FABRIC.

You'll have the best luck using drapey fabrics with high stability and a tight weave, such as crepe.

## FORGET THE BIAS.

Another possibility is simply not to bother with the bias. Try using the pattern on the straight grain with a knit fabric or a woven fabric with a bit of horizontal stretch.

**1.** Trace and cut the patterns for the front and back bias skirt from sheet 3 back. See the note on page 150.

**2.** Cut the fashion fabric according to the cutting layout. With right sides together, sew the back pieces together at the center back. *Note:* If you are using a back zipper, leave the top 8" (20.5cm) of the seam from the waist open.

**3.** With right sides together, sew one side seam. Sew the other side seam to within 8" (20.5cm) of the waist, leaving the rest of the seam open for the side zipper. Make sure the open seam is on the same side as your open bodice seam. If you prefer a back zipper, sew both side seams and leave the back open.

**4.** Clip the curves (page 36) and press the seams open.

**5.** Hem the bottom of the skirt with either a 1" (2.5cm) blind hem stitch (page 24) or a rolled hem. Lighter fabrics like chiffon work best with a rolled hem. For a rolled hem, press the raw edge to the inside by ¼" (6mm) and then stitch ⅛" (3mm) from the folded edge. Trim the seam allowance very close to the stitching line and then press to the inside again by ¼" (6mm); stitch close to the folded edge.

**6.** If you plan to fully line the final dress, repeat all steps with the lining fabric but make the lining ½" (13mm) shorter than the dress so it won't peek out when moving.

**7.** See page 32 for how to attach the skirt to the bodice.

## MODIFICATIONS FOR STEP 1

**1.** You can modify the bias pattern to remove the train by drawing a straight line and slashing to the hem. For a smoothly curved hemline, adjust the center-back hem, making the last ¼" (6mm) or so at the center back perpendicular.

**2.** To make this modified trainless pattern for a side zipper instead of a back zipper, cut off the ⅝" (1.5cm) center-back seam allowance.

*brunch in paris dress*
# THE SIX-PANEL SKIRT

Whether it's at a sidewalk café in the City of Lights or in your own hometown, you will find plenty of opportunities to wear this dress. The flared hem of the six-panel skirt creates a graceful silhouette, and the skirt's seams mimic those of the princess bodice (page 98), lending this dress a tailored look. These instructions are for the six-panel skirt with a side zipper. If you'd like this as a stand-alone skirt, see page 187 for how to make a waistband.

## PATTERN PIECES

Center Front 6-Panel (sheet 2 front)
Side Front 6-Panel (sheet 2 front)
Center Back 6-Panel (sheet 2 front)
Side Back 6-Panel (sheet 2 front)

## YARDAGE

FASHION FABRIC AND LINING FABRIC
1½ yards (1.4m) of 45" (114cm) or 60" fabric, all sizes

## SUPPLIES

invisible zipper

### notes
- *Use a ⅝" (1.5cm) seam allowance for all sewing.*
- *If you prefer a back zipper, add a ⅝" (1.5cm) seam allowance to the Center Back 6-Panel pattern. In that case, instead of cutting 1 center back panel on the fold as shown in the cutting layout, you will cut 2 separate pieces for the back of the skirt.*
- *The zipper length should be 8" (20.5cm) plus the length of the bodice center-back seam for a back zipper or the length of the bodice side seam for a side zipper.*

## FABRIC TIP

In order for the flared bottom of the six-panel skirt to hang correctly a lightweight, drapey, languid fabric should be used. See page 14 for more about fabrics.

## CUTTING LAYOUT

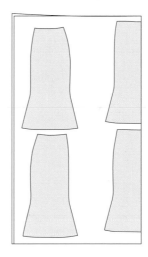

**1.** Trace and cut the pattern pieces for the six-panel skirt from sheet 2 back. Cut the fashion fabric according to the cutting layout.

**2.** With right sides together, sew one side front panel to the center front panel. Repeat with the other side front panel. Press the seams open.

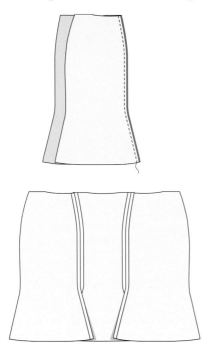

Repeat with the back panels.

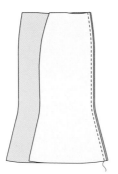

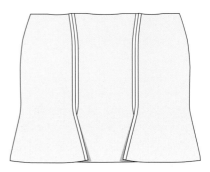

**3.** With right sides together, sew the front to the back along one side seam. Sew the other side seam to within 8" (20.5cm) of the waist to leave room for the zipper. Make sure to leave the same seam open for the zipper as you did on your bodice.

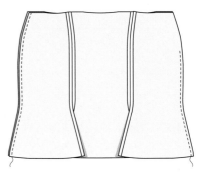

**4.** Hem by pressing the bottom edge of the skirt to the inside by ¼" (6mm). Press to the inside again by ⅜" (1cm) and stitch close to the folded edge. See page 23 for more about hemming.

**5.** If you will be fully lining the dress, repeat all steps with the lining fabric but make the lining ½" (13mm) shorter than the skirt so it won't peek out.

**6.** See page 32 for how to attach the skirt to the bodice. See page 33 for how to insert the zipper.

*eyelet sundress*

# THE DIRNDL SKIRT

**Everyone needs a summery white dress for casual gatherings and weekend getaways. The full dirndl skirt is just as easy to sew as it is to wear. This eyelet dress would make a great addition to any summer wardrobe. These instructions are for the gathered dirndl skirt with a side zipper. It's shown in the sample with the mock-wrap bodice (page 95). If you'd like this as a stand-alone skirt, see page 187 for how to make a waistband.**

**YARDAGE**

dependent on your measurements and desired skirt length

**SUPPLIES**

invisible zipper

**notes**

- *The zipper length should be 8" (20.5cm) plus the length of the bodice center-back seam for a back zipper or the length of the bodice side seam for a side zipper.*
- *The amount of fabric the skirt requires depends on the fullness and length you desire. For heavier, thicker fabrics, you may want fewer gathers, up to 1½ times your waist measurement, as too much fabric will be bulky at the waist and more difficult to gather. For thin, lightweight fabrics, it all depends on the look you want. Twice the waist measurement or even more can work well with lighter weight fabrics.*
- *These directions are for a stand-alone skirt drafted to your waist measurement. If you will be attaching the skirt to a bodice, measure and use the waist measurement of the front and back bodice, excluding seam allowances, in place of your waist measurement when calculating the total skirt width.*

**FABRIC TIP**

This skirt will work well with many different types and weight of fabric. See page 14 for more about fabrics.

1. **For a skirt with two side seams,** cut 2 rectangles from your fashion fabric that are 1½–2 times your waist measurement plus 1¼" (3cm) for the side seam allowances plus a ½" for wearing ease for the width by your desired length plus 2⅝" (7cm) for the waist and hem seam allowances. For example, for a skirt that is 24" (61cm) long with a 26" (66cm) waist and lots of gathers (double the waist measurement) you would calculate as follows:

*for the width*:

26" (66cm) waist measurement × 2 = 52" (132cm)

52" (132cm) ÷ 2 = 26" (66cm)

26" (66cm) + 1¼" (3cm) + ½" (13mm) = 27¾" (70.5cm)

*for the length*:
24" (61cm) + 2⅝" (7cm) = 26⅝" (68cm)

So in this case, each fabric rectangle would be 27¾" (70.5cm) wide × 26⅝" (67.5cm) long.

**For a one-seam skirt,** cut a fabric rectangle that is twice your waist measurement plus 1¼" (3cm) for the seam allowance plus 1" (2.5cm) for wearing ease by desired length plus 2⅝" (7cm) for the waist and hem seam allowances.

**2.** Loosen the thread tension of the upper thread on your machine. This will make gathering easier. Sew 3 rows of basting stitches at the top edge of your fabric: 1 just a tiny bit above the ⅝" (1.5cm) seam allowance (the stitching line) and 2 more above that toward the raw edge of the seam allowance. Three rows of stitching ensure that if one thread breaks while gathering, you have two more threads to work with.

Gently gather each rectangle along the three threads to half your waist measurement plus 1¼" (3cm) for the side seam allowances.

**3.** Tighten the thread tension back to a normal setting. With right sides together, sew one side seam. Make sure not to catch any gathers in the seam. Sew the other side seam up to 8" (20.5cm) from the waistline to leave room for the zipper. Make sure to leave the same seam open for the zipper as you did with your chosen bodice. Press the seams open.

**4.** Press the hem to the inside by 1" (2.5cm), repeat, and sew close to the folded edge or use a blind hem stitch (page 24) for a less conspicuous finish.

**5.** If you would like to line the skirt, repeat all steps for the lining but make the lining ½" (13mm) shorter so that it doesn't peek out from under the skirt.

**6.** See page 32 for how to sew the skirt to the bodice. See page 33 for how to insert the zipper. See page 187 for how to attach a waistband if you prefer a stand-alone skirt.

*perfect day for a picnic dress*
# THE PLEATED SKIRT

This dress is as classic as a wicker picnic basket and a red-checkered blanket. The simple, sleeveless bodice allows the pleated skirt to take center stage, while the skirt's longer length is perfect for windy days in the great outdoors. These instructions are for the pleated skirt shown with the basic bodice (page 49). The amount of fabric it requires depends on your desired fullness and length.

### YARDAGE

dependent on your measurements and desired skirt length

### SUPPLIES

invisible zipper

**notes**

• *The zipper length should be 8" (20.5cm) plus the length of the bodice center back for a back zipper or the length of the bodice side seam for a side zipper.*

• *These instructions are for a pleated skirt that is attached to a bodice. For a stand-alone skirt use your waist measurement plus 1" for wearing ease in place of the bodice waistline measurement when calculating the total fabric width.*

### FABRIC TIP

The pleated skirt will work with many different fabrics but a nonslippery fabric with a bit of stiffness will be easier to work with and press into pleats.

1. For a continuous one-seam skirt with 1" (2.5cm) pleats, measure the front and back waist of the basic bodice pattern (don't include the seam allowances) and multiply by 3. Each completed pleat will require 3" (7.5cm) of fabric, so if the waistline of your bodice measures 26" (66cm), for example, your fabric would need to be 78" (198cm) wide plus 1¼" (3cm) for the seam allowances by your desired length plus 2⅝" (7cm) for the waist and hem allowances.

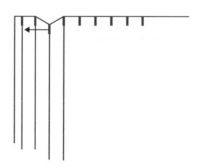

2. Make a mark on what will be the waist of the skirt with tailor's chalk or a dressmaker's pencil ⅝" (1.5cm) from the edge. Mark every 1" (2.5cm) along the waist from this point.

**3.** Pinch the fabric together and pull it up at the 3rd mark and bring it over to meet the 1st mark. Press and pin in place. Pinch together at the 6th mark and bring it over to meet the 4th mark. Press and pin. Pinch together at the 9th mark and bring it over to meet the 7th mark. Continue in this way down the waistline. Leave ⅝" (1.5cm) unpleated at the end for the seam allowance.

**4.** Machine-baste just inside (closer to the raw edge) the ⅝" (1.5cm) seam allowance along the waist of the skirt to secure the pleats.

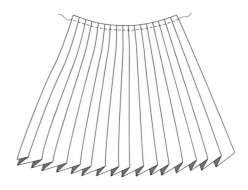

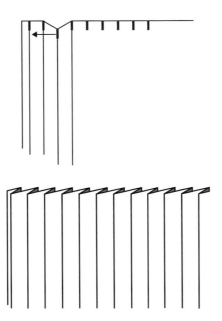

**5.** With right sides together, sew the back seam of the skirt, leaving 8" (20.5cm) open toward the waistline for the zipper. Press the seam open.

**6.** Press the hem inside by 1" (2.5cm), repeat, and sew close to the folded edge or use a blind hem stitch (see page 24).

**7.** See page 32 for how to sew the bodice to the skirt and page 33 for how to insert the zipper. Or for a stand-alone skirt, see page 187 for how to attach a waistband.

# valentine's day dance dress
# THE BOX-PLEAT VARIATION

Not just for Valentine's Day, this full-skirted style would be perfect at any event that calls for a slightly whimsical look. The box pleats give the skirt a distinct style with a very constructed look. It is made in a similar way to the pleated skirt. It is shown with the basic bodice modified with an all-in-one sleeve (page 145), the deep V-neck (page 112), and a Johnny collar (page 120).

### YARDAGE

dependent on your measurements and desired skirt length

### SUPPLIES

invisible zipper

**note**
• *The zipper length should be 8" (20.5cm) plus the length of the bodice center back for a back zipper or the length of the bodice side seam for a side zipper.*
• *See page 187 for how to make a waistband for a stand-alone skirt.*

### FABRIC TIP

The box pleats work well in medium-weight fabrics with a bit of stiffness and body. See page 14 for more about fabrics.

**1.** Follow steps 1 and 2 for the pleated skirt on page 163.

**2.** Pinch the fabric together and pull it up at the 3rd mark and bring it over to meet the 1st mark. Pinch and pull the fabric up at the 5th mark and bring it over to meet the 7th mark. Pinch and pull the fabric up at the 9th mark and bring it over to meet the 7th mark. Pinch it up at the 11th mark and bring it over to meet the 13th mark. Continue in this way down the waistline. Leave ⅝" (1.5cm) unpleated at the end for the seam allowance.

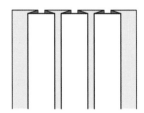

**3.** Follow steps 4–7 for the pleated skirt to complete the box-pleat skirt.

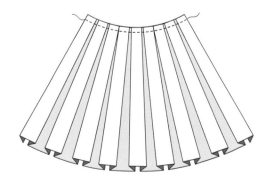

*simply chic dress*

# THE STRAIGHT SKIRT

A strapless bodice (page 73) paired with a straight skirt is a flattering, yet easy-to-sew silhouette. Lace with some stretch makes this party-perfect, but don't be afraid to imagine it in a more casual cotton print or a more dramatic fabric like black dupioni silk. These instructions are for the straight skirt with a side zipper and back vent. If you'd like to make this as a stand-alone skirt, see page 187 for how to make a waistband.

## PATTERN PIECES

Front Straight Skirt (sheet 1 back)
Back Straight Skirt (sheet 1 back)

## YARDAGE

**FASHION FABRIC AND LINING FABRIC**
45" (114cm) fabric:
• Size 1: ¾ yard (68.5cm)
• Sizes 2 to 12: 1½ yard (1.4m)
60" (152.5cm) fabric
• Sizes 1 to 10: ¾ yard (68.5cm)
• Sizes 11 and 12: 1 yard (0.9m)

## SUPPLIES

invisible zipper

### notes
• *This skirt can be made with a back zipper instead without modifying the pattern.*
• *The zipper length should be 8" (20.5cm) plus the length of the bodice center back for a back zipper or the length of the bodice side seam for a side zipper.*
• *To make the skirt without the vent simply extend the back seam line to the hem and cut off the vent extension. Unless you're using a very stretchy fabric, it will be difficult to walk in the skirt without some sort of opening at the hem. You can make a simple slit by leaving about 8" of the back seam open from the hem. Press the slit seam allowance to the inside and finish with lace hem tape.*

## FABRIC TIP

The straight skirt will work best with a medium- to heavier-weight fabric with a bit of body. It will also work with a fabric with a bit of stretch. See page 14 for more about fabrics.

## CUTTING LAYOUTS

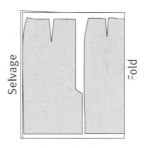

45" (114cm), size 1
60" (152.5cm), sizes 1–10

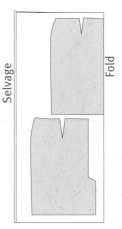

45" (1.4m), sizes 2–12

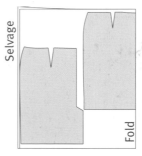

60" (152.5cm), sizes 11 and 12

1. Trace and cut the pattern for the Front and Back Straight Skirt from sheet 1 back.

2. Cut the fashion fabric according to the appropriate cutting layout for your fabric width and size.

3. Sew the back darts and press toward the center. Serge or zigzag-stitch (page 22) the straight edge of the vent extensions.

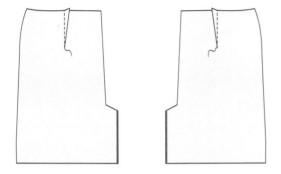

4. Sew the front darts. Press toward the center.

5. With right sides together, sew the back skirt pieces together from the center back waist and along the top edge of the vent extension.

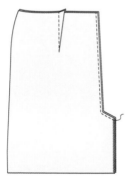

6. Cut a notch at the intersection of the back seam and the vent extension.

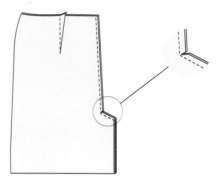

7. Press the back seam open. Press the vent extension to one side. Stitch the vent diagonally along its top edge to the skirt.

8. With right sides together, sew the back of the skirt to the front along one side seam. Sew the other side seam, where the zipper will be inserted, to within 8" (20.5cm) of the waist. Make sure to leave the same seam open for the zipper as you did for the bodice. Press the seams open.

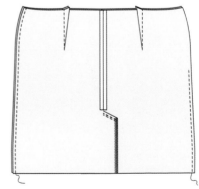

**9.** Unfold the vent extension and press the hem to the inside by 1" (2.5cm). Repeat and sew close to the folded edge or use a blind hem stitch (page 24). Make a few hand stitches through the edge of the folded vent extension through one layer of the fold of the hem to secure.

# skirt modifications

Like the Basic Bodice pattern (page 49), the basic Straight Skirt pattern can be easily modified by slashing and spreading to create patterns for an A-line skirt, a skirt with fullness at the hem, a panel skirt, and a gathered skirt as well as a wrap skirt.

To make all of these modifications to the back skirt pattern, you must first cut off the vent extension and the ⅝" (1.5cm) back seam allowance.

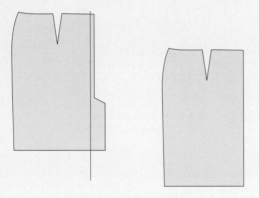

The modified pattern would now be cut on the fold of fabric to create a skirt with side seams and no back seam for the zipper. If you prefer a back zipper to a side zipper add the ⅝" (1.5cm) back seam allowance when you're done modifying the pattern and cut 2 separate pieces, not 1 on the fold.

## A-LINE SKIRT

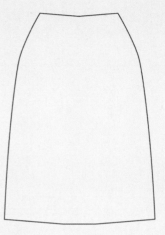

The A-line skirt

**1.** Trace the Front Straight Skirt pattern from sheet 1 back. Draw lines from the tip of the dart to the hem.

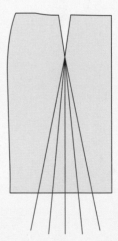

**2.** Slash the lines, leaving hinges. Spread the slashed pieces evenly and rotate the side seam piece upward to close the waist dart. Trace the new pattern. Repeat with the back skirt pattern.

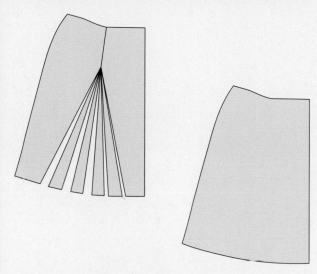

**note** *You can do this modification using just a single slash and closing the waist dart. The dart space opened up at the hem will be exactly the same either way. The advantage to doing it this way, however, is that, when spread out, all those smaller slashed pieces give you a more accurate sense of how to draw the new hemline. Depending on your figure, you may want to flatten the hipline of the A-line pattern by slashing from the side, waist to hem.*

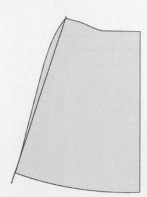

How to flatten the hip line for an A-line skirt

# FULL-HEM SKIRT

**1.** Start with the Front and Back A-Line Skirt pattern described on the opposite page. Draw straight lines that are equally spaced along the waist and hem. The more lines you draw, the more accurate the new hemline curve will be, though too many lines may become difficult to work with especially if using lightweight paper. Slash the lines from the hem, leaving small hinges at the waist.

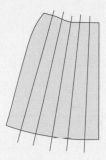

**2.** Spread the pieces evenly. Spread the center front of the skirt half the amount of the other pieces and trace the new pattern.

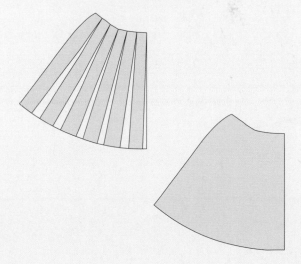

# TWELVE-PANEL SKIRT

You can make fewer or more panels as you wish.

**1.** Start with the Front and Back Full-Hem Skirt pattern described on page 173. Mark and cut off the ⅝" (1.5cm) seam allowance along the side seam. Divide into equal parts at the waist and hem with straight lines.

**3.** You may also want to mark the pieces as center front/back, middle front/back, and side front/back for clarity. Slash the lines. Add a ⅝" (1.5cm) seam allowance along each slashed edge and along the center front and side seam panel.

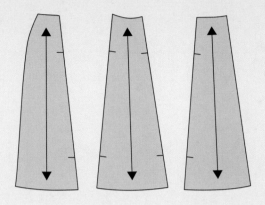

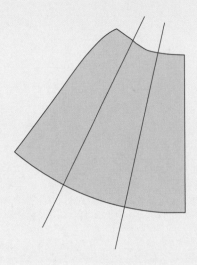

**2.** Draw an arrow through the middle of each panel to indicate the grain line and mark notches on each piece to indicate where to match and sew them together.

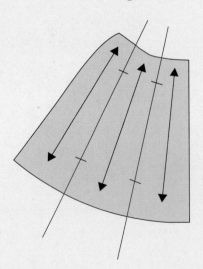

# FULL-HEM GATHERED SKIRT

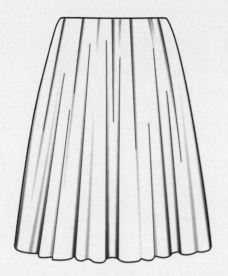

The gathered full-hem skirt

When you'd like to have fullness and gathers without too much bulk at the waist, the A-line or full-hem gathered skirt is a great option.

**1.** Start with the pattern for the A-line (page 172) or Full-Hem Skirt (page 173). Draw straight lines through the skirt, dividing the waist and hem equally.

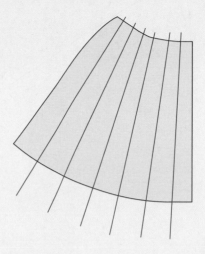

**2.** Slash and spread the lines vertically, making sure to space them evenly. Trace the new pattern.

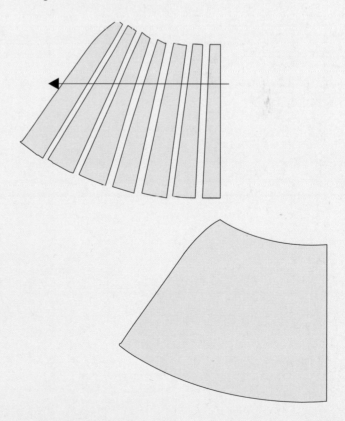

# WRAP SKIRT

**1.** Use the Front and Back Straight Skirt patterns modified to an A-line (page 172) or an A-line with a fuller hem (page 173).

**2.** Cut 2 front pieces from the fashion fabric and 1 back piece.

**3.** With right sides together, sew 1 front piece to the back piece. With right sides together, sew the other front piece to the back.

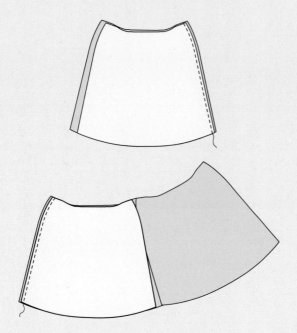

**4.** Cut a waistband that is 2½ times your waist measurement by 3¼" (8.5cm) wide.

**5.** Press the short ends of the waistband to the wrong side by ⅝" (1.5cm). Press the long edges of the band to the wrong side by ⅝" (1.5cm).

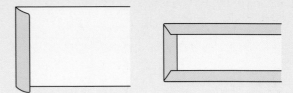

**6.** Press the sides of the skirt to the inside by ¼" (6mm), repeat, and stitch close to the folded edge.

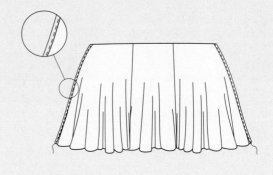

**7.** With right sides together, align the raw edge of the waistband with the top of the skirt and sew.

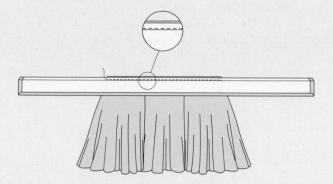

**8.** Fold the band over the raw edge of skirt so that the folded-under edge of the waistband aligns with the stitching line. Sew the waistband to the skirt from the inside, very close to the folded edge. Sew the ties in the same way.

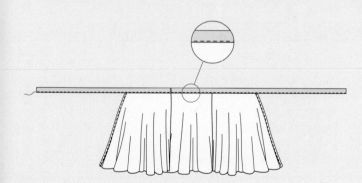

**9.** Make a buttonhole (page 34) in the waistband near one side seam for the tie to pass through.

**10.** Press the hem to the inside by ½" (13mm). Press to the inside again by ⅜" (1cm) and stitch close to the folded edge.

## *diane wraparound dress*
# THE A-LINE WRAP VARIATION

Revolutionary designer Diane von Furstenberg forever changed fashion when she debuted her little wrap dress in the '70s. It's surprisingly easy to convert the mock-wrap bodice (page 95) into a true wrap dress that ties with an attached fabric belt. Though shown here in a sleeveless variation, I can also envision this dress combined with long sleeves (page 134) and an attached Johnny collar (page 120).

**notes**
- *For the mock-wrap bodice, use the yardage amounts and cutting layouts on page 95.*
- *Yardage for the skirt is variable, depending on how much fullness you've added to the skirt.*

**1.** Start with the Mock-Wrap Bodice pattern (sheet 2 back) and the Front and Back A-line Skirt patterns modified from the Straight Skirt pattern (page 178). You'll also need the Back Basic Bodice pattern (sheet 1).

**2.** Trace the front A-line pattern. Flip it over, line it up with the center front of the tracing, and trace again to make a complete Front A-line Skirt pattern.

**3.** Measure the Mock-Wrap pattern, not including the dart, at the waist. Measure out from the side seam along the waist of the complete A-line pattern the same amount. Make a straight line at this point from the waist through the hem that is parallel to the side seam. Slash the pattern along the line to complete the front wrap pattern.

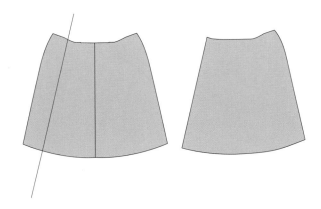

**4.** Cut 2 front wraps and 1 back A-line skirt from your fashion fabric. Cut 2 mock-wrap bodice pieces and 1 back bodice piece from your fashion fabric.

**5.** Sew the mock-wrap darts and press toward the center. Sew the back bodice darts and press toward the center.

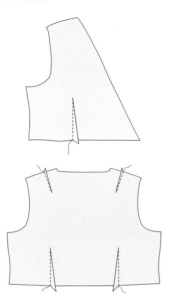

**6.** Sew the front bodice pieces to the back at the side seams only. Press the seams open.

**7.** Sew the 2 front skirt pieces to either side of the back skirt piece with right sides together. With right sides together, sew the bodice to the skirt, making sure the side seams are aligned. Press the seams open.

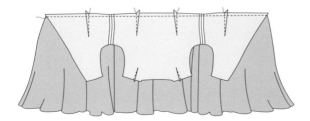

**8.** Arrange the dress so that the shoulders are aligned with right sides together, and sew the shoulder seams.

**9.** Make the pattern for the front facing by tracing the front closing edge of the dress. Make the facing at least 2 ⅝" (7cm) wide where possible. Make the patterns for the front and back armholes and back neckline facings using the patterns (see page 25). Cut the facing fabric and interfacing using the facing patterns. Interface the wrong side of the facing fabric according to the manufacturer's instructions (see page 31 for more on interfacing).

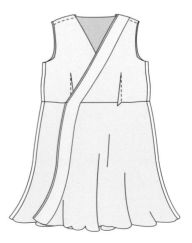

**10.** Sew the front facings to the back neckline facing at the shoulders with right sides together. Sew the front and back armhole facings with right sides together at the shoulder and underarm seams. Press the seams open.

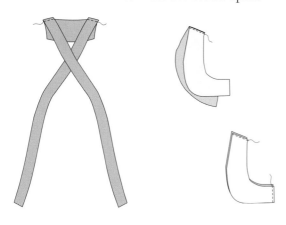

**11.** Sew the armhole facing to the dress with right sides together. Sew the neckline facings to the dress with right sides together but leave 1¼" (3cm) unsewn at the waist on both sides for the ties. Make a buttonhole (page 34) near the waist and the side seam of the bodice.

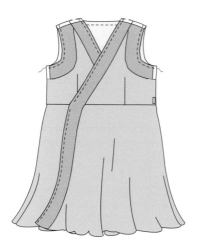

**12.** Cut 4 strips of fashion fabric 2¼" (5.5cm) wide for the ties; make sure they are long enough to wrap around your waist and tie in a bow or knot (approximately 2.25 times your waist measurement). Press 1 short end of each strip to the wrong side by ¼" (6mm). With the folded-under short ends aligned, sew 2 strips with right sides together along each long edge. Repeat with the other 2 strips. Turn right side out using a safety pin and press.

**13.** Place a tie in between the facing and dress with raw edges aligned at the waist and sew. Repeat on the other side of the dress with the remaining tie.

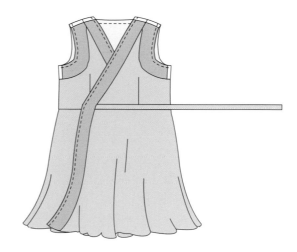

**14.** Grade the seams (page 35), clip the curves (page 36), understitch the bodice seam allowance to the facing (page 36), and finish the seam allowances (page 36), if desired. Press the facings to the inside of the dress.

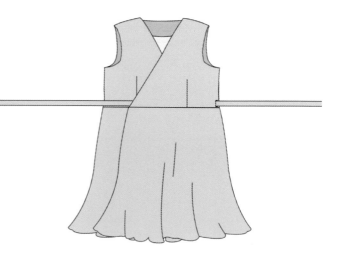

*first anniversary dress*
# THE CIRCLE SKIRT

An important date calls for a special dress, so spring for a fabric with exquisite drape. The effect will be well worth the effort of handling a trickier fabric. Circle skirts are great for many styles, from casual to business to party. They have the advantage of being full at the hem but slim without any bulk at the waist, yielding an elegant silhouette. Here you'll find instructions for drafting a full, three-quarter-, half-, and one quarter-circle skirt to your own measurements.

## YARDAGE

Depends on the size of final pattern

## SUPPLIES

Invisible zipper

### notes

• *Unlike other kinds of skirts, circle skirts are not made from different front and back patterns. Rather, the front and back are cut in the same way. They can also be made with a single seam, eliminating front and back altogether.*

• *The zipper length should be 8" (20.5cm) for a stand-alone skirt. For a skirt sewn to a bodice, it should be 8" (20.5cm) plus the length of the bodice center back for a back zipper or the length of the bodice side seam for a side zipper.*

• *Some parts of a circle skirt will necessarily be cut on the bias (see page 152 for more about the bias). This means the skirt will stretch around the body but also downward. It's a good idea to hang your uncut fabric on the bias for a few days before sewing your skirt to let it do as much downward stretching as possible. After you've sewn your skirt, hang it again for a couple more days before hemming it. Then, put the skirt on yourself or a dress form. You may find the hem is uneven as it has stretched downward at the bias portions but not at the straight-grain portions. To mark the hem evenly, lay the skirt on a flat surface. Use a yardstick to measure and mark down from the waist the desired length plus hem allowance around the hem. Trim the hem where it has stretched beyond this length.*

## FABRIC TIP

Circle skirts work beautifully with all types of fabrics. A very drapey fabric will yield a languid, close-to-the-body look. A stiffer fabric will stand away from the body, more like a classic '50s poodle skirt.

*draft the pattern*

note *If you are making just a skirt without a bodice, use your waist measurement to draft the skirt. If you are making the skirt to join one of the bodices in the book, measure the stitching line (⅝" [1.5cm] in from the pattern edge) of the front and back bodice pattern waistline (don't include the seam allowances) and use that for the waist measurement.*

### FULL CIRCLE SKIRT

1. Draw a rectangle ¼ the waist measurement wide (waist = full waist minus 1" [2.5cm] to compensate for bias stretching) by the desired length. Slash it into equal parts, the more the better, almost but not quite through the waistline. Spread as shown on the right angle of another piece of paper. Trace the curved shape. *Note:* This will result in a pattern that is ¼ of the full skirt.

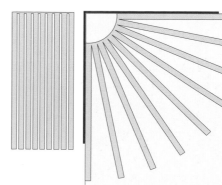

**2. For a two-seam skirt:** Mark 1 straight edge as the center front. Add ⅝" (1.5cm) seam and hem allowances to the other edges. Cut 2 pieces with the center front on the fabric fold.

**For a one-seam skirt** (which requires a large piece of fabric): Cut 2 pattern pieces and tape them together to form ½ of the full pattern. Add ¼" (6mm) seam allowance to the straight edges and ⅝" (1.5cm) seam allowance to the both waist and hem. Cut 1 on the fabric fold. Then cut a straight line from the waist to the hem in order to create a seam where the zipper can be inserted.

**TIP**

*You can also make a panel skirt from the full-circle skirt pattern. Create the pattern as described on page 183. Divide the pattern into equal parts with straight lines from the waist to the hem. Slash the lines. Add ⅛" (1.5cm) seam and hem allowances to all edges. Cut 4 of each panel from fabric.*

### HALF-CIRCLE SKIRT

**1.** Draw a rectangle ½ the waist measurement wide (waist = full waist minus 1" [2.5cm] to compensate for bias stretching) by the desired length. Slash into equal parts, the more the better, almost but not quite through the waistline. Spread as shown on the right angle of another piece of paper. Trace the curved shape. *Note:* This will result in a pattern that is ½ of the full half-circle skirt.

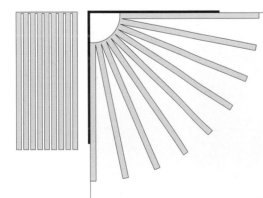

**2. For a two-seam skirt:** Add ⅝" (1.5cm) hem and seam allowances to all edges. Cut 2 from the fabric.

**For a one-seam skirt:** Mark 1 straight edge as the center front. Add ⅝" (1.5cm) seam and hem allowances to the other edges. Cut 1 with the center front on the fabric fold.

### QUARTER-CIRCLE SKIRT

**1.** Draw a rectangle ½ the waist measurement wide (waist = full waist minus 1" [2.5cm] to compensate for bias stretching) by desired length. Slash into equal parts, the more the better, almost but not quite through the waistline. At the corner of another piece of paper, fold one edge over to meet the other edge.

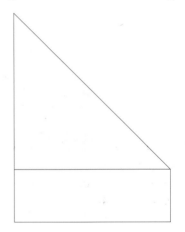

**2.** Unfold the paper. Spread the slashed piece as shown on the 45-degree angle formed by the fold. Trace the curved shape. *Note:* This will result in a pattern that is ½ of the full quarter-circle skirt.

**3. For a two-seam skirt:** Add ⅝" (1.5cm) seam and hem allowances to all edges. Cut 2 from fabric.

**For a one-seam skirt:** Mark 1 straight edge as center front and add ⅝" (1.5cm) seam and hem allowances to other edges. Cut 1 with the center front on the fabric fold.

## THREE-QUARTER-CIRCLE SKIRT

**1.** Draw a rectangle that is ¼ the waist measurement wide (waist = full waist minus 1" [2.5cm] to compensate for bias stretching) by the desired length. Slash into equal parts, the more the better, almost but not quite through the waistline.

**2.** At the corner of another piece of paper, fold 1 edge over to meet the other edge, forming a 45-degree angle. Fold once more to find the 67.5-degree angle.

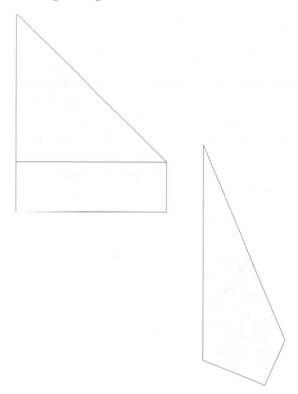

**3.** Unfold the paper and spread as shown on the 67.5-degree angle formed by the fold. Trace the curved shape. *Note:* This will result in a pattern that is ¼ of the full three-quarter-circle skirt.

**4. For a two-seam skirt:** Mark 1 straight edge as the center front. Add ⅝" (1.5cm) seam and hem allowances to other edges. Cut 2 with the center front on the fabric fold.

**For a one-seam skirt** (which will require a large piece of fabric): Cut 2 pattern pieces, tape them together, and mark 1 straight edge as center front. Add ⅝" (1.5cm) seam and hem allowances to other edges. Cut 1 with the center front on the fabric fold.

**SEWING INSTRUCTIONS FOR ALL CIRCLE SKIRTS**

**1.** With right sides together, pin and sew the seam(s). Leave the top 8" (20.5cm) from the waist of one seam open for the zipper. Make sure the open seam is on the same side as your bodice. Press the seams open.

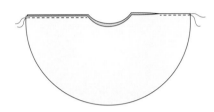

**2.** Fold the edge of the skirt to the inside by ¼" (6mm) and press. Stitch the hem ⅛" (3mm) from the fold. Trim the seam allowance close to the stitching (page 23). Fold over again by ¼" (6mm) and stitch close to the folded edge. Finish seam allowances (page 36), if desired. See page 32 for how to sew the skirt to the bodice.

## Waistband for a Stand-Alone Skirt

1. To make a 1" (2.5cm) waistband for a stand-alone circle skirt (or any of the other skirts in this chapter), cut a strip from your fashion fabric that is 2" (5cm) plus 1¼" (3cm) for the seam allowances wide by the length of the waistline of the finished skirt plus 1" (2.5cm) for the button-tab overlap.

2. Press the open portion of the side seam of the skirt to the wrong side by ⅝" (1.5cm) on both sides of the seam. See page 33 for how to insert the zipper (not shown). In this case, the top of the zipper where the teeth end should be aligned ⅝" (1.5cm) down from the skirt waist. The zipper tapes will end up covered by the band. Press the short ends of the band strip to the wrong side by ⅝" (1.5cm). Press one long edge to the wrong side by ⅝" (1.5cm). Align

the unpressed raw edge of the band to the raw edge of the waist of the skirt with right sides together. Make sure that it is positioned so that the button overlap is extending (with the seam allowance folded in) past the side seam of the skirt. Pin and stitch in place.

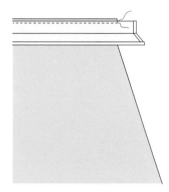

3. Flip the band over the raw edge of the skirt. Make sure the band's raw edge is folded under and is aligned with the stitching line. Pin and stitch close to the folded edge on the inside of the skirt and on the short end of the tab. Make a buttonhole in the tab (page 34) or use a hook-and-eye closure.

# ·6·
# fittings and alterations

THERE ARE ENTIRE BOOKS DEVOTED TO THE SUBJECT OF FITTINGS and alterations. A detailed discussion of it is beyond the scope of this book, but I felt a book about fitted dresses needed to include the basics. After all, no matter how lovely the design is, if the dress doesn't fit you correctly, you won't want to wear it. This primer will help you identify common fitting problems and show you how to alter a pattern to fix them.

You may know from your own experience with ready-to-wear clothing or sewing patterns what fitting problems you tend to have. If so, it's best to alter the pattern using the alteration techniques discussed before you do anything else. Or, if unanticipated problems come up when you make the muslin, you can use the following techniques to alter the pattern.

# BASIC PATTERN ALTERATIONS

Before starting your pattern alterations, it's a good idea to mark all of the pattern stitching lines ⅝" (1.5cm) in from the cut edge. Measurements taken on your body (wearing the undergarments you would wear with a dress) need to be compared and adjusted to the pattern as it will be sewn; therefore, the seam allowances need to be omitted from any and all measurements.

Generally, do all vertical (lengthening and shortening) alterations first. The exception is the small/large bust adjustment on the front bodice, in which length and width are adjusted simultaneously. Height does not dictate whether a garment needs to be lengthened or shortened. Tall people can have a long torso, therefore needing to lengthen only the bodice and not the skirt, and short people may have long legs, so may need to shorten the bodice while lengthening the skirt. It's all about proportion.

# TORSO LENGTH ADJUSTMENTS

**1.** Place a length of narrow elastic around your waist, and bend from side to side to get it to settle. Your natural waist is higher than most people think, usually 3" (7.5cm) above your belly button, and is generally the smallest measure between your bust and your hips. Most people don't wear their pants there, but it is a very flattering place for the waistline of a dress.

**2.** Measure your center-back length, from the nape of your neck straight down to the elastic. Compare it to the length of the pattern's bodice back, remembering not to count the seam allowances. If the difference in measurements is less than ½" (13mm), you're fine. More than that

and you'll want to draw a line perpendicular to the grain line, across the back bodice, just below the armpit. Spread or overlap the line evenly to achieve the correct back length.

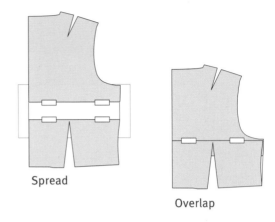

Spread

Overlap

**3.** Redraw lines if needed by blending the pattern lines at the overlap or spread. For preliminary front adjustments, you need to lengthen or shorten the front bodice the same amount as you did the back bodice.

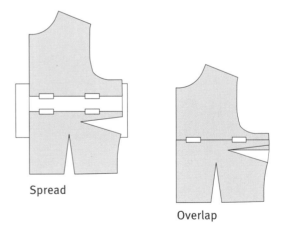

Spread

Overlap

# BUST ADJUSTMENTS

All standard bodice patterns are made for a B-cup bra size. If you are smaller or larger than a B cup, and/or your bust sits higher or lower than average, then you'll want to adjust your pattern before you start to get a better fit.

**1.** With the elastic still around your waist, look in a mirror and measure vertically from your shoulder, over the fullest part of your bust, and down to your waist. The bodice front needs to be this long to fit properly. Also note the measurement along that line, where the apex of your bust (or bust point, basically your nipple) sits. You'll need this to mark an accurate bust point on your pattern.

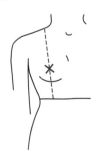

**2.** Measure from side seam to side seam, across the fullest part of your bust. Add 1" (2.5cm) for wearing ease. Divide in half (because the pattern is half of the front). Also note the distance from the side seam to the bust point.

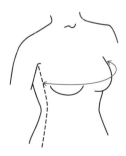

**3.** On the front bodice pattern, locate the pattern's bust point by drawing straight lines through the center of each dart. Where they intersect is the pattern's bust point. Mark the bust point on the pattern and mark the dotted lines as pictured. Cut along each of these lines, leaving only a small hinge at the armhole and, for the large bust adjustment, also at the bust point to pivot the pieces. For a small bust adjustment cut through the bust point.

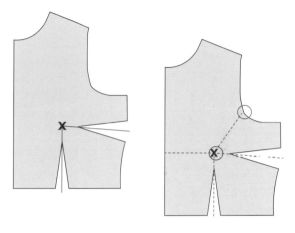

**4.** Working on a flat surface, spread or overlap the pattern pieces as shown until the length and width measurements you took earlier are achieved. Keep the waistline of the bodice even and the center-front line even. A general rule will be to increase/decrease length and width about ½" (13mm) per change in cup size. For instance, a D cup will add about 1" (2.5cm) in length and width. Tape the altered pattern in place.

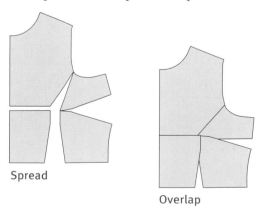

Spread

Overlap

**5.** Mark the correct bust point on the pattern as you measured on yourself earlier, both the height (as measured from your shoulder) and the width (as measured from the side seam). Mark new waist and bust dart points as follows: The point of the waist dart will be 1" (2.5cm) directly below your new bust point. The side dart point will be 1" (2.5cm) away from your bust point, in the direction of the dart (to the side and slightly down). Connect these new points to the end of the legs of the original darts, which have now spread (for larger cups) or overlapped (for smaller cups). Redraw pattern lines smoothing out any bumps or jags caused by the alteration.

In cases where the corrected bust point is lower than the side dart end points, the side dart end points will also have to be lowered. Measure the distance that the bust point was lowered. Lower the end points of the dart legs the same distance, taking care to lower them vertically. In other words, move the entire side dart downward, not just the tip, on the spread-out or overlapped pattern. This keeps the width of the front bodice consistent. Draw in the new dart legs, lowering the tip of the waist dart the same amount the bust dart was lowered on the spread or overlapped pattern.

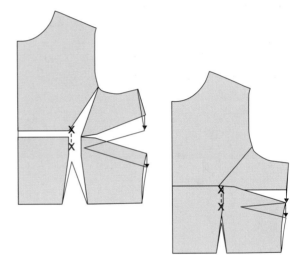

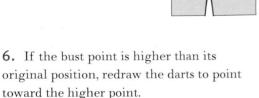

**6.** If the bust point is higher than its original position, redraw the darts to point toward the higher point.

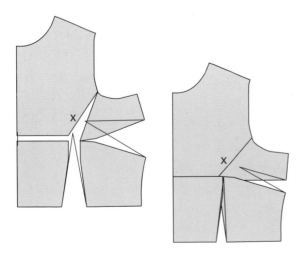

**7.** To complete the pattern, redraw the side seam by connecting the new dart legs with the armhole and the waistline for the spread or overlapped pattern.

## NECK ADJUSTMENTS

If the neckline is too tight or too loose, adjust the pattern accordingly.

**1.** Measure around your neck where you'd like the finished neckline to sit. Divide the measurement in half as you are working with half the pattern.

**2.** Mark the stitching lines for the neck and shoulder on both the front and back bodice, ⅝" (1.5cm) in from the cutting edge. Line up the shoulder stitching lines and tape in place. Don't worry about the shoulder dart. Measure the stitching line for the neck by holding a soft, flexible tape measure on its side (that is, standing up on its thin edge), not flat, around the neck stitching line. Hold it so the increments are against the pattern for the most accurate measure.

Marked stitching lines

**3.** For every 1" (2.5cm) difference between the stitching line and the target measure, move the pattern's neckline ¼" (6mm) at the center front and at the shoulder line, either in, toward the neck to make it smaller, or out, away from the neck to make it bigger. For example, if you want to increase the neck 1" (2.5cm), you'll move the center-front point down ¼" (6mm) and the shoulder line out ¼" (6mm). Keep the center back the same. Redraw the neck stitching line,

and double-check the pattern measure. Add the ⅝" (1.5cm) seam allowance to the stitching line. Adjust again if needed.

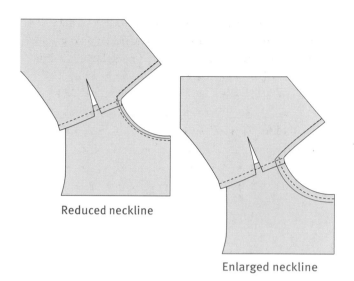

Reduced neckline

Enlarged neckline

## SHOULDER ADJUSTMENTS

### SHOULDER SLOPE CORRECTION

This method will correct for wide or narrow shoulders, as well as square or sloping shoulders.

**1.** Have a friend measure across your back, from shoulder point to shoulder point, where sleeve seams would sit. This is your shoulder width. Divide this by 2, since the pattern is for half of the back. Then, with the elastic around your waist, have a friend measure from your waist at center back, to your shoulder point, where a sleeve seam would sit. This is the shoulder slope.

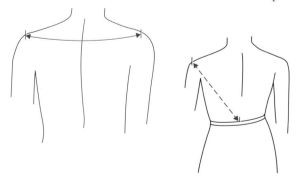

**2.** Compare your shoulder width (that you've divided by 2) to the bodice back, omitting the seam allowances. If you're within ¼" (6mm), you'll be fine. If not, you'll want to correct for shoulder width. Do this before correcting for shoulder slope. Draw a horizontal guideline, parallel to the waist, through the shoulder point. Starting at center back, measure along this line to your target shoulder width. Make a mark on the line. Next, draw a vertical line through your mark, keeping it perpendicular to the waistline to mark the wider or narrower shoulder.

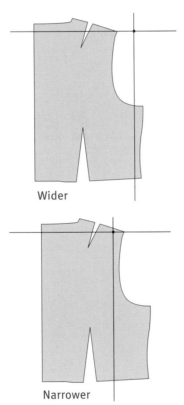

Wider

Narrower

**3.** Starting at the waist at center back, mark where your shoulder-slope measure crosses the vertical line. This is your new shoulder point. Note how far above or below the original shoulder point this is, as you will need to adjust the armhole this same amount. Draw your new shoulder line from this point to the neck.

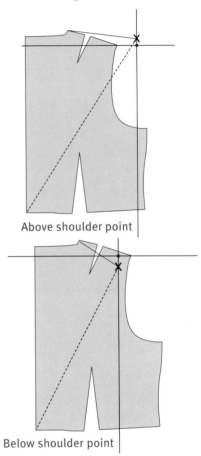

Above shoulder point

Below shoulder point

**4.** Find the midpoint of your new shoulder line. This will be the center of your shoulder dart. At the midpoint, draw a line perpendicular to your shoulder line that is the same length as the original dart. This is your dart center, and the end is your dart point. Measure the width of the original dart. Mark the dart width on the shoulder line with the perpendicular line in the center. Draw in your dart legs, connecting these marks to the end of the perpendicular line.

**5.** Correct the armhole as needed:

**If your shoulder width was adjusted, but not the shoulder slope,** redraw your armhole, starting at the shoulder, and blend back into the existing armhole about midway down the curve for the wider or narrower shoulder.

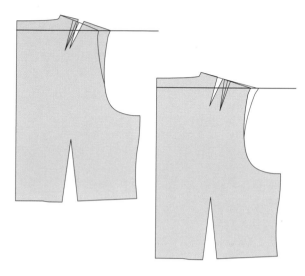

**If your shoulder slope was also changed,** draw a vertical guideline at the outer point of the armhole/side seam, perpendicular to the waist. Mark a new point along this guideline up or down—the same amount that you raised or lowered the shoulder point. This keeps the armhole the same size. To redraw this line, try to mimic the bottom of the curve through the midpoint of the curve. Then blend to your new shoulder point for a wider or narrower shoulder.

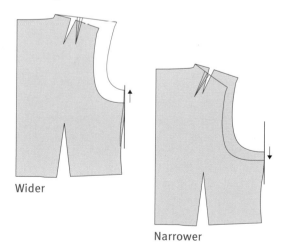

Wider

Narrower

**6.** Apply the same changes to the front bodice: Draw a horizontal guideline through the front bodice shoulder point. Move the shoulder point in or out the same amount that you moved the back shoulder. Draw a vertical line through this new point. Now raise or lower the shoulder point the same amount that you raised or lowered it in the back, to correct for shoulder slope. Connect this mark to the original neckline. Redraw the armhole as in step 5.

**7.** When you change the armhole on the bodice, you then must change the armhole on the sleeve so it still fits into the bodice. For shoulder width adjustments, you may or may not need to adjust the armhole, depending on the changes. Measure the original armhole stitching lines on the back bodice. Now measure your new armhole on your back bodice, along the stitching lines. The difference between the two measurements is the amount that you will raise or lower the sleeve cap. If your new armhole is bigger than the original armhole, you will raise the sleeve cap by that same amount. If your new armhole is smaller than the original armhole, you will lower the sleeve cap by that amount.

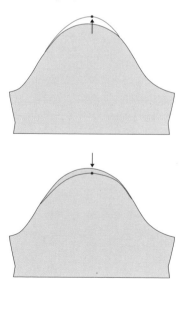

## ROUNDED SHOULDERS

For figures with rounded shoulders, there are often gaping armholes in the back, and when viewed from the side, the shoulders are forward from the neck and the back is more prominent than the front.

**1.** Have a friend measure from the crease in the flesh above the armpit, across your back, to the crease above your other armpit. Have your friend take the same measurement across your front.

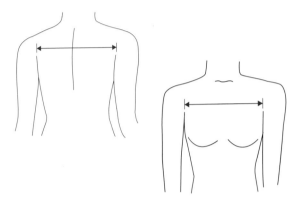

**2.** If the front measurement is 1½" (3.8cm) or less than the back, no change is needed. For differences greater than 1½" (3.8cm), make the following corrections: On the back bodice, draw a horizontal guideline through the center of the armhole curve. Then extend the center line of the dart through the horizontal line. Cut along both of these lines, leaving a small hinge of paper at the intersection. Place new paper behind the dart, as it will spread and you'll want something to tape it to.

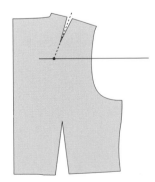

**3.** Take your back measurement and subtract the front measurement. Divide this number by 2 to get the width of the shoulder dart needed to shape the back properly. For instance, if the back measure is 15" (38.5cm) and the front measure is 13" (33cm), then 15 minus 13 is 2, and 2 divided by 2 is 1; therefore, the dart needs to be 1" (2.5cm) wide. Rotate the outer shoulder piece of the pattern downward until the shoulder dart is the target width, overlapping the cut at the armhole. Tape in place. Using the original dart length, mark a new point near the center of where the paper has spread and connect it to the dart legs. Redraw the armhole to smooth out the overlap. Measure the amount that the pattern is now overlapped at the armhole.

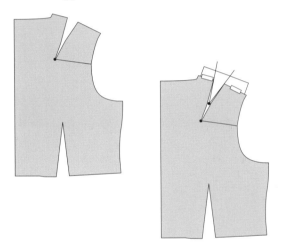

**4.** Now the front. As the shoulders move forward, the armhole in the front also needs to move forward. On the bodice front, draw a horizontal guideline across the center of the armhole. Along the guideline, mark inward, toward the center front, the amount of the overlap you measured on the back. Redraw the armhole by blending into the shoulder point and along the bottom curve. The resulting curve will have a lower, more pronounced curve than before.

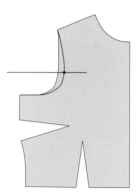

**5.** Because we changed the shape of the armhole, we want to change the shape of the sleeves so that they will still fit together nicely and hang properly on the body. On your sleeve pattern, draw a horizontal line midway through the cap between the front notch mark (one notch) to the back notch marks (two notches). Draw 2 more horizontal guidelines, 1 touching the top of the cap and 1 at the beginning of the underarm seam. Using the overlap measurement taken previously, you will decrease the sleeve cap in the back, increase the sleeve cap in the front, and move the shoulder point (notch at the top of the shoulder curve) forward. Redraw the lines, blending into the lower curves and the top of the sleeve cap.

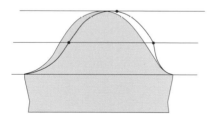

## SLEEVE ADJUSTMENTS

### SHORTEN OR LENGTHEN SLEEVES

**1.** Measure your arm from the shoulder point to the wrist and compare to the pattern. Draw a horizontal guideline through the sleeve, keeping it perpendicular to the grain line. Cut along this line.

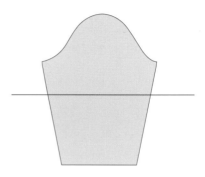

**2.** Spread the pattern over another piece of paper to lengthen it or overlap to shorten until the target length is reached; tape. Do not include seam allowances in the measurement. Be careful to keep the grain aligned. Redraw the seam lines (true up) smoothing out any jags.

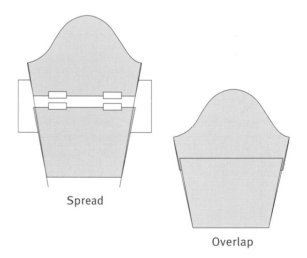

Spread

Overlap

## UPPER ARM CORRECTION

**1.** Measure your bicep at its fullest part. Add 2" (5cm) for wearing ease; you may add more for personal preference, but in woven fabric, a 2" (5cm) minimum is needed. This is the total width that your sleeve should be. Also note how far down from the shoulder seam you took this measurement.

**2.** On your sleeve pattern, draw the following guidelines: (a) a horizontal guideline at the level where you took your bicep measurement (from the shoulder point); (b) a vertical line from the shoulder-point notch through the hem, and (c) a horizontal line through the end points of the shoulder curve. Leaving small hinges of paper right at the stitching lines, cut along all lines, except the bicep guideline.

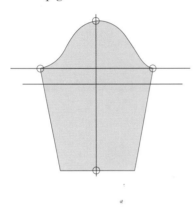

**3.** Spread the pattern to add width or overlap to reduce width until the target measurement is reached (don't include the seam allowances) along the horizontal bicep line. Tape in place. Redraw to smooth the sleeve-cap curve and redraw the hem so that it's straight. Redraw the grain line.

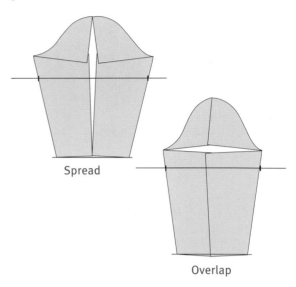

Spread

Overlap

## OVERALL ARM CIRCUMFERENCE CORRECTION

**1.** Take bicep measure following step 1 of Upper Arm Correction. Also take a forearm measurement at the fullest part of your forearm. Add at least 1½" (3.8cm) of wearing ease for this measure. Also note how far down the arm (from the shoulder point) you took this measurement.

**2.** On your sleeve pattern, draw horizontal lines that correspond to your bicep and forearm. Then draw a horizontal line through the end points of the shoulder curve. Lastly, draw a vertical line from the shoulder-point notch down through the hem. Leaving hinges at the shoulder point and the sleeve end points, cut along these last 2 lines.

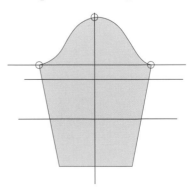

**3.** Spread the pattern to widen or overlap to reduce width, checking along the bicep line and forearm line for the target measurement. It's fine if either the bicep or forearm measures are bigger than the target, just not both of them. Tape in place. Redraw to smooth the sleeve-cap curve. Straighten the hem if necessary. Double-check the length of the sleeve and adjust if needed, as instructed above.

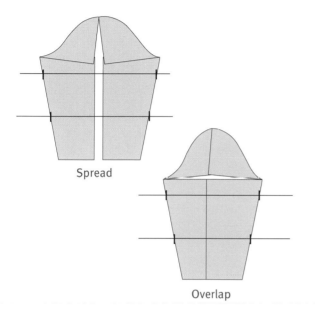

Spread

Overlap

## SKIRT ADJUSTMENTS

### SKIRT LENGTH ADJUSTMENTS

It's best to lengthen or shorten a skirt from the middle of the pattern in order to preserve any hem details (like a kick pleat) and the fullness in the hem.

**1.** Measure from your waist to the length you would like the skirt. Compare to the pattern. Draw a line perpendicular to the grain line at about the hipline level.

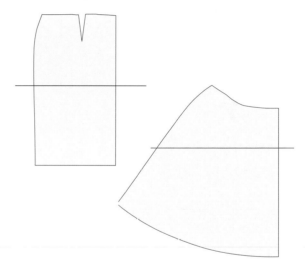

**2.** Cut and spread the pattern to lengthen it, or overlap to shorten.

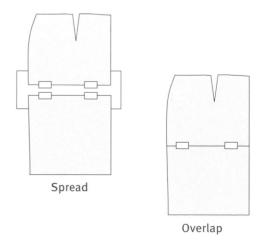

Spread

Overlap

**3.** Tape in place, and redraw the pattern lines smoothing them out as you do. Don't forget to make the same adjustment on both front and back skirt pattern pieces.

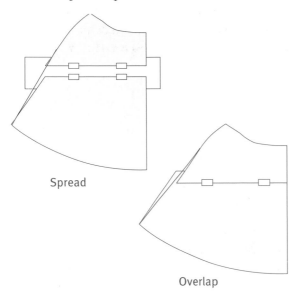

Spread

Overlap

## SWAYBACK ADJUSTMENT

**1.** If posture is such that the back (in profile) has a significant arch, there often is rippling at the center-back waist when wearing dresses or skirts. For this alteration, place elastic snugly around the waistline and parallel to the floor (when viewed from the side), and have a friend measure the distance from the center-back waist at the elastic to the floor. Then measure from the elastic at the center-front waist to the floor. The back measurement will be greater than the front measurement with a swayback. Subtract the front measurement from the back. This is the amount of the swayback adjustment.

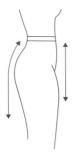

**2.** Measure down along the center-back seam of the skirt pattern the amount needed for adjustment. To redraw the waistline, start at the center-back waist and draw a slight curve that is perpendicular to the center-back seam at the start and curves up to join the original waist at the side seam.

**3.** The newly drawn curve will have crossed the back dart, which will now need to be enlarged to maintain the original waist size. On the original waist seam, measure from the center back to the first dart leg. Now measure along the *new* waist seam, starting from the center back, and mark this first measurement. On the original waistline, starting from the side seam, measure over to the other dart leg and mark this measurement on the new waistline. The space left in between your marks will be the new dart. Draw a new center line for the dart centered between the marks, the same length as the original dart, and perpendicular to the new waistline. Draw your new dart legs, connecting the marks to the end of the center dart line.

**4.** Take your original swayback adjustment from step 1 and add it onto the hem at center back to correct the hem length. Redraw your new hemline, blending back to the original line at the side seam.

## HIPS OR THIGHS CORRECTION

**1.** Measure all the way around the fullest part of your hips or thighs (whichever are fuller). Add 2" (5cm) for wearing ease. Divide by 4 (since each pattern piece is one fourth of the full pattern). Also measure how far down from your waist this measurement was taken. On both the front and back skirt pieces, measure the same amount down from the waist and draw a horizontal line to represent your hipline. Then, starting from center front or center back, measure across to your target width and mark inside the original side seam for a smaller hip or outside for a larger hip. Remember not to include the ⅝" (1.5cm) seam allowance when you do this.

**2.** Redraw the side seam and blend the new hip point to the waist seam and to the hem. Add the ⅝" (1.5cm) seam allowance to your new side seam.

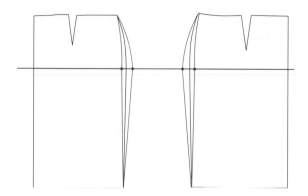

## SEAT CORRECTION

**1.** Measure from side seam to side seam across the fullest part of your seat. Add 1" (2.5cm) for wearing ease and divide by 2. This is your target measurement. Also measure how far down from your waist you took this measurement. And measure from the center back to the first dart leg along the waistline of the pattern.

**2.** On the back skirt pattern, measure down from the waist the same amount you measured on yourself in step 1. Draw a horizontal line to be your new hip (seat) line at this level. Also draw a vertical line through the center of the dart to the hem. Cut all the way along this vertical line.

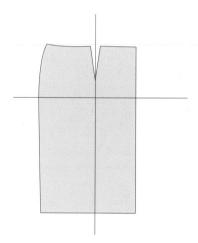

**3.** Spread or overlap the skirt pattern, keeping the grain lines straight, until the target measurement is reached along the hipline. Tape in place.

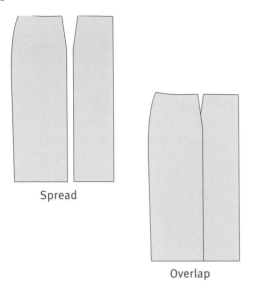

Spread

Overlap

**4. For a small seat:** If the dart legs are at least ½" (13mm) apart, use a dart length of 3½" (9cm) measured through the center of the dart perpendicular to the waist, and draw in new legs.

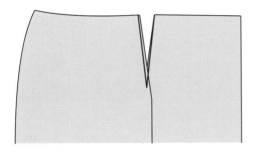

If the dart has closed or overlapped, you will need to put in a dart and add length to the waistline to accommodate the new dart. Using the original measurement of the pattern waistline (omitting seam allowances and the dart) measure and mark this distance along your waistline. Now add ¾" (2cm). Blend this into the original hipline. To make the new dart, make a mark on the waistline the same

distance from the center back as the first dart-leg measurement you took in step 1. Draw a 3½" (9cm) line perpendicular to the waistline ⅜" (1cm) away from the mark toward the side seam. Make another mark ⅜" (1cm) away from the perpendicular line toward the side seam. Connect the marks to the end of the perpendicular line to form your new dart.

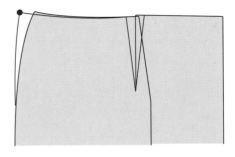

**For a large seat:** Find the midpoint of your dart. From there, measure 6" (15cm) downward, perpendicular to the waistline, and make a mark. Connect the dart legs to this point to form your new dart.

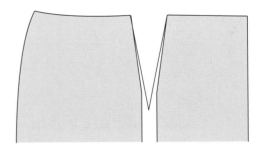

# acknowledgments

Thank you to my husband for supporting me through another book! I know it wasn't easy, so thank you, my love.

Thank you to my children, Max, Harry, and Ava, for being wonderful young humans and for being so much fun to just hang out with and talk to. I love you like crazy and am so proud of each of you.

Thank you to my mother, Linda Whelan, and my father, Tom Whelan, for always supporting me. Love you both so much.

Thank you to my uncle Barry Becker, a technical-illustrations machine! Just a few more, I promise. Love you, ub.

Thank you to Bob and Allen for your patience, professionalism, and good cheer. I could not have completed this successfully without you! Thank you both so very much.

Huge, giant thanks to Barbie McCormick, couture dressmaker and expert pattern designer extraordinaire. The lady with the answers! Thank you, Barbie, for absolutely everything. You gave me the confidence to complete this project. If you're looking to have a special custom dress designed and made, Barbie is the lady to talk to. Please contact her at barbiemccormick.com.

Thank you to Sew Boise. Visit them at sewboise.com.

Very special thanks to alteration and dressmaking expert Sandra Hutton of the Seamstress for making all those dresses (!), for helping me style the models so beautifully, and for your moral support and assistance with the shoot. I will always be grateful to you for your help with his project. Contact Sandra at (717) 243-0753 for expert alterations and dressmaking.

Thank you to Colleen Mohyde for making this project happen and keeping it (and me) going through the rocky parts!

Thank you to my editors, Caitlin Harpin and Emma Brodie, for your help and patience in making this project come to fruition in a beautiful way.

Thank you to the beautiful (inside and out) models who brought the dresses to life. I couldn't have asked for a more lovely or professional group of women to work with.

Thank you to Silva!

# fabric resources

**Fabric.com**
Great variety of apparel fabrics often at a discounted price

**Etsy.com**
Wonderful for beautiful vintage fabrics

**Moodfabrics.com**
Ranges from reasonably priced high-quality blends and synthetics to expensive high-end designer, silk, lace, and wool fabrics

**Girlcharlee.com**
A variety of high-quality knit fabrics, especially ponte

**Joann.com**
A dependable resource for a variety of apparel fabrics, especially basics such as lining fabrics, at a good price

**Fatquartershop.com**
Huge selection of printed cotton fabric

# about the author

Tanya Whelan is well known for her fresh, vintage modern style. Her bestselling fabrics and sewing patterns are produced and distributed internationally by Free Spirit Fabrics, a subsidiary of Coats & Clark. Her scrapbooking and paper designs are distributed through Trimcraft. Her work is featured frequently in magazines, including *Martha Stewart Living*, *Romantic Homes*, *Quilts and More*, *Sew News*, and *Mollie Makes* as well on the blogs *Decor8*, *Sew Mama Sew*, *True Up*, and *Craftzine*. She lives in the United States with her husband and three children. Visit Tanya at grandrevivaldesign.com.

# index